A HISTORY OF THE CELTS

By the same author

A HISTORY OF THE CELTS

Horace E Winter

The Book Guild Ltd
Sussex, England

First published in Great Britain in 2004 by
The Book Guild Ltd
25 High Street
Lewes, East Sussex
BN7 2LU

Typesetting in Times by
Acorn Bookwork Ltd, Salisbury, Wiltshire

Printed in Great Britain by
CPI Bath

A catalogue record for this book is available from
The British Library.

ISBN 1 85776 867 1

*This book is dedicated to the memory
of my father and mother.*

CONTENTS

FOREWORD

The history of the Celts is a massive subject which could fill many volumes. In presenting this shorter history the author hopes that it will encourage readers to seek further information from the specialised books on this subject which are available in public libraries and many of which are included in the bibliography in this book.

The Celts did not have a written language and all tribal records were memorised and passed on from one generation to another. This lack of written records made it very difficult to get a clear picture of their life and culture and it was almost a lost civilisation until the mid 1800s when amazing discoveries at Hallstatt and La Tène revealed for the first time evidence of their culture throughout Europe, the British Isles and Ireland and linked together the many isolated discoveries in these areas. The Celts occupied a huge territory which stretched from the Rhine to the Pyrenees and from Romania to Ireland. Their weakness was that they always adhered to their separate tribal existence. There are between 13 and 14 million Celtic people and each Celtic region produced its own flag and emblem.

The only remaining areas of Celtic language and culture are Brittany, Cornwall, Wales, Scotland, the Isle of Man and Ireland. All these areas have societies which are very active in not only preserving their language and culture, but in promoting it, especially amongst children.

Thorneycroft,
Blindcrake.

ACKNOWLEDGEMENTS

The author is very grateful for the help and friendly assistance readily given by the following, and for the documents and photographs which they supplied, and for their permission to make use of these, and wishes to thank them for making it possible to write this book.

Dr R. H. Bewley, Air Survey Officer, Royal Commission of Historical Monuments.

The *Conservateur de Musée Cantonal d'Archeologie de Neuchatel*, Switzerland.

The Austrian National Tourist Office, London.

The *Landesmuseum für Kärnten*, Klagenfurt, Austria.

Herr K. Wirobal, Custodian, Hallstatt Museum, Austria.

Dr H. P. Uenze, *Prähistorische Staatssammlung*, Munich.

Miss F. Devlin, Education Officer, National Museum of Ireland, Dublin.

The Western Regional Tourism Organisation Ltd, Galway-Mayo, Eire.

John and Moira Bowyer, for Irish information and photographs.

Andrew Foxon, Assistant Keeper, Department of Archaeology, Ethnography and History, Glasgow Museum.

Jean Yves Veillard, *Conservateur de Musée de Bretagne*, Rennes, Brittany.

Iceland Tourist Board, Reykjavik, Iceland.

Director of Tourism, Orkney Tourist Board, Kirkwall, Orkney.

W. M. M. Horn, Deputy Director and Dr L. S. Garrad, Assistant Keeper, The Manx Museum, Douglas, Isle of Man.

Colin Richardson, Keeper of Archaeology, Tullie House Museum, Carlisle.

Joan Caine, Hon. Secretary, The Manx Gaelic Society, Peel, Isle of Man.

Wella Brown, General Secretary, The Cornish Language Board, Saltash, Cornwall.

The Spanish National Tourist Office and Institute of Spain, London.

Donald J. Macleod, Education Officer, *Comunn na Gaidhlig* (Scottish Gaelic Society), Inverness.

D. M. MacLean, Organising Secretary, *An Comunn Gaidhealach*, Stornoway, Isle of Lewis.

The Cornwall Tourist Office.

The Isle of Man Department of Tourism, Douglas.

The Wales Tourist Board, Cardiff.

Shetland Tourist Organisation Information Centre, Lerwick, Shetland.

The Irish Tourist Board, London.

The Scottish Highlands & Islands Guide.

Joanne Hillman, Librarian, Redruth Library, Cornwall.

Joyce Foster, County Reference Library, Truro, Cornwall.

The Staff of Cockermouth Library and the Travelling Library.

Dr Kilian and Carola Kreilinger, Munich.

G. Olafsson, National Museum of Iceland, Reykjavik.

Dr R. Ködderitzsch, University of Bonn.

Bulletin of the Department of Foreign Affairs, Eire.

Senor J. M. Garcia, *Oficina de Informacion de La Coruna*, Galicia, Spain.

Senor don F. Senén, Keeper of the *Museo Arqueológico* of Castillo de San Antón, La Coruna, Galicia, Spain.

The Librarian, Manx Reference Library, Douglas, IoM.

The Librarian, Public Lending Library, Douglas, IoM.

Senor E. P. Canamares, *Museo Arqueológico Nacional*, Madrid, Spain.

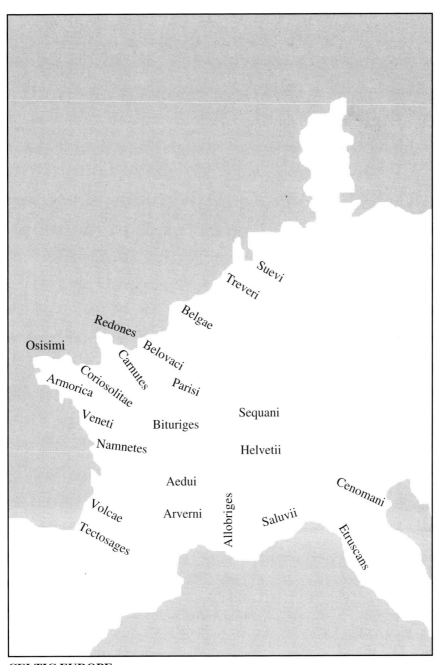

CELTIC EUROPE

1

The Beginnings

After the Ice Age small groups of nomadic people began to appear and they existed first as hunters and collectors of wild berries and fruit and, later, as small communities producing their own food. These immigrants came from many eastern and southern Russian areas, spreading through Bohemia and coming up from Persia and later using ponies for transport.

By 4,500 BC agricultural settlements had spread across Europe as far as Holland and by 3,000 BC they had established themselves in France and Britain.

The Late Stone Age spans from 3,400 BC to 1,600 BC and these Neolithic people lived in Central and Northern Europe and developed the stone axe, first tied on to a handle and then fixed to a handle by a hole in the axe head. By 2,500 BC immigrants from South Russia to the Danube, Rhine, Belgium and Holland improved on it and by 1,500 BC the stone axe began to give way to one of copper or bronze.

By 3,000 BC clay pots began to be used in the Black Sea region and were ornamented by pressing cords into the soft clay. About 2,500 to 2,000 BC a beautifully made bell-shaped pot, red in colour, was being produced in Spain and the North African coastal regions. This pot has been found in Neolithic graves throughout Europe and Britain.

In 1,500 BC they buried their dead in barrows under mounds of earth, either in small groups, singly or communally, or in large cemeteries. These mounds have been found in Bavaria, Bohemia, Switzerland, Burgundy, Belgium and Britain. A barrow grave in South Russia contained a silver vase. These are known as Tumulus people.

In Poland, Silesia, Saxony and Bohemia it was the custom to cremate and bury the remains in urns in large cemeteries. These are known as Urnfield people. It was the custom to bury the possessions of the dead with them and sometimes horses were buried with them too.

The Emergence of the Celts

Neolithic man migrated to Britain from NE France and the earliest migrations of Celts to Britain in the Bronze Age were from France and the Low Countries. By 700 BC large migrations had begun and by the early part of the 5th century BC stronger migrations took place. These included the Celtic tribe of the Pretani, from whom the name 'Britain' derived, the 'Pretanic Islands'.

The Celts emerged, first in Austria, Southern Germany and Switzerland, where their highest standards were achieved, and they spoke a common tongue – Celtic. Their methods of cultivation and crop growing gradually improved, as did their metal working, which resulted in new tools and weapons. The new tools enabled them to clear more and more ground for agricultural purposes.

The name 'Celtic' is linguistic rather than tribal. Some Celts were tall and fair, others were small and dark, but they all had the same basic root form of language, that is why they were all called Celts.

The Celtic language descended from a common mother tongue known as Aryan. It is thought it originally came from the Hamitic tongue, Egyptian, Barber, Kabyle etc., the North African white race known as the Iberians, who have left their megolithic monuments along the routes of their migrations in Spain, France, Britain and Ireland.

When the Celts imposed their language on the language of the original inhabitants, certain idioms survived.

It was first during the Romanisation of the Celtic tribes (43–426 AD) that the Celtic tongue lost its purity and adopted many Latin words, indeed some districts adopted the Latin speech completely.

When, during the following 500 years, when occupations were made by various foreign invaders, the Celtic tongue largely disappeared, and only survived in a few places, in Ireland, Wales, Cornwall, Scotland, the Isle of Man and Brittany.

At one time Breton and Cornish spoke the same language, and Welsh was very similar. Now all three have their own languages.

It has been spoken in Great Britain for more than 3,000 years, probably commencing in the Bronze Age and being added to in the Iron Age.

The former are called Goedelic, and the latter Brythonic. The Goedelic Celts have survived in the Highlands and Islands of Scotland, Ireland and the Isle of Man, and the Brythonic Celts in Wales, Cornwall and Brittany. It is thought Irish was introduced into Scotland and became the Scottish form of Gaelic, as spoken today.

In Brythonic 'qu' appears as a 'p' sound. In Goidelic it remains 'q'.

The Greeks were curious to know more about the 'barbarians' in Europe, whom they called *Keltoi*, from which the name Celts came. Their writers recorded what they could find out about them. In the early 6th century BC it was recorded that the Celts lived in the North Sea area, in France and Spain. Ephorus in the 4th century BC states that in Europe were the Scythians and Celts. Hecataens in 500 BC writes of the Celtic towns of Narbonne and Nyrax. Later Herodotus states that Celts lived in the upper Danube Valley, near the Pyrenees and in Spain.

By 600 BC the Celts occupied most of Europe from Austria to the Atlantic coast.

The Celts were a brilliant, brave and intelligent people, but undisciplined and foolhardy, with no military organisation. They frequently squabbled and fought each other and proved no match to the organised military might of the Romans, although they were very skilful with their cavalry and war chariots, which the Romans regarded with great respect. The Romans called them *Galli* (Gauls). Strabo wrote, 'At any time or place, you will find them ready to face danger, even if they have nothing on their side but their own strength and courage.'

They liked to wear neck rings, and bracelets on their arms and wrists, but finger rings were seldom worn. Men, women and children wore the neck rings (torcs), the better-off gold ones, either solid, hollow or twisted, the less well-off wore bronze ones, whilst the poor had to make do with iron ones. They spiked out their hair with limewash.

They lived mainly on milk and pork. Hares, fowl and geese were unlawful to eat.

Iron axes came into use from the 7th century BC and forests were more rapidly cleared then. In the 6th century BC they reaped two harvests in a single year. They grew rye, club wheat and chess, as well as beans, also emmer, spelt, millet, barley and oats. Wild animals and fish were also caught.

Their fields were square or sub-square from one third to one and a half acres. They would plough a field in a day using an iron-shod plough drawn by two oxen. Cattle were shorthorn, sheep were small, and the wool was plucked not shorn. Pigs were kept and ponies bred and they had dogs and cats. In the Paris area it was mainly sheep and goats and in the north cows. Crops were harvested with knives and sickles and hauled on four-wheeled carts or sledges. They stored their grain in pits, sealed with clay, or in huts raised on stilts. Grain was ground in rotary querns. Butter and cheese were made. Wool was spun and woven into cloth, looms being used with bone combs. Increased food production meant an increase in population.

Hurdles were made. Tubs, cups and ladles were made of wood, as well as ladders, doors, spade and knife handles. They made beams and planks, used mortice and tenon jointing and doweling. They used saws, awls and bill hooks. Antlers were also used for handles and bridle-cheek pieces. Bone was used for flutes and horns. Dice were made from polished pebbles and dice boxes were also made. Braids for ornamental borders on clothing were produced from bone tablet weaving.

Hill sites were chosen for forts or settlements, often on older sites built in pre-Celtic times. (In Britain are 3,000 Iron Age hillforts.) Some of these older forts were as early as the 9th century BC, and were constructed on earth and timber. German Celts introduced the stone faced ramparts. These fort settlements could contain up to 3,000 people.

Iron smelting was done in shallow bowl furnaces. Iron ore was mixed with charcoal and heated. A spongy mass of iron called bloom was left and had to be re-heated and beaten. Iron ore was collected from shallow surface workings. Iron ingots were used at times as currency. Salt was produced from sea water which was run into large pans.

They wore tunics with trousers and used cloaks. The men were clean shaven but had long hanging moustaches.

When going into battle they wore helmets and used shields and their arms were swords and spears and slings using pebbles or clay shot. The shields were made of wood or wickerwork and sometimes covered with leather. Wives had the right to accompany their husbands into battle and take part in it, as they were familiar with the martial arts. Their war chariots were pulled by two ponies in a double yoke. A charioteer drove the ponies whilst the warrior took part in combat, usually leaving the chariot to take part in hand-to-hand fighting and returning to the chariot if his efforts were successful. The charioteers were very skilful in handling the ponies. The Celts had war trumpets and when going into battle made a great noise and also banged their shields and gave vent to war cries. The horses of defeated enemies were sometimes drowned or sacrificed.

Their Religion and Customs

The Celts worshipped many gods and 69 names of gods are known, some of which are – Latis, Tentates, Ollondius, Segoma, Lenus, Corotlacus, Lenuminus, Alator, Loucetius, Nemetius, Regisamus, Nodons, Cammlos, Brociaca, Belatucadros, Barrex, Medocius and Condatis.

They revered rivers and named them after goddesses, as well as springs, wells, ponds and lakes and made votive offerings to them, throwing into them clothing, food, metal work, weapons, tools, ornaments and coins. (Coventinas's Well in Northumberland was found to contain over 14,000 coins etc.) The River Seine in France, was named after the Goddess Sequanna. At its source, in 1963 200 carved wooden votive objects were found.

Deep shafts were dug and votive offerings were cast into them to appease the underworld gods. Many shafts have been found in Bavaria.

The Celts lived under Druidical law. The Druids were priests, teachers, healers, poets, musicians and judges. They were under the control of an Arch-Druid appointed by his fellow Druids. If there were more than one candidate, elections were held. They were a privileged class and were exempt from military duty and taxes. Training for the priesthood was very rigorous due to the great volume of oral learning which they had to memorise, as they had no written language, so it could take up to 20 years to complete their studies. They had to learn them in simple verse form. They were only recruited from the ruling classes. There were three classes of Druids. There were Bards, poets who delivered eulogies in song, on the history and traditions of the tribe. There were the Augerers, who saw to the sacrifices and who foretold the future and there were the Druids, who were versed in law and philosophy. They settled all disputes and crimes and their decisions were final. They were astronomers and had to be present at all sacrifices, which were both human and animal. They taught that the soul does not perish, but after death passes from one body to another and this encouraged bravery in battle. They believed that the soul was in the head and this led to a head cult. Sometimes the heads of important enemies slain in battle were cut off by the Celts. Some were preserved in cedar oil, others were deposited in temples, or erected outside their own dwellings. They believed that in possessing the head they had complete control of the person. This cult was strongest in the Marseilles area. Some heads were thrown down votive shafts, as well as stone carved heads. At Entremont in Provence, France, the Salii tribe had a sanctuary to the head cult up to the Roman conquest.

The Celts were very superstitious and believed spirits abounded around them in the natural world. Over 400 names are recorded. The torc was worn around the neck to ward off evil spirits.

The oak tree was considered sacred, as was mistletoe when it grew upon it. A priest would cut it off with a golden sickle, on the sixth day of the moon. They then held an animal sacrifice at the foot of the tree. They worshipped in oak groves. The yew tree was also sacred. They venerated the raven, swan, bull, stag, bear, boar and horse. The goose, cock and hare were also sacred.

The Celtic New Year feast on the 1st November (Samain), now Hallow'en, was when stock was slaughtered. The 1st February (Imbole), marked the beginning of the lactation of ewes. On the 1st May (Beltain), the cattle were turned out to graze. Two large bonfires were lit and the cattle were driven between them, to protect them from disease. The 1st August (Lugnasad) was when the ripening of the crops was celebrated.

A large proportion of the Celts belonged to the poorer class. The land belonged to the clan as a whole. Those who possessed stock were freemen. They had the right to bear arms and take part in the general assemblies which could elect or dispose of a king. The nobility were in control of the assemblies. Leases were granted on livestock. The annual rent was equal to one third of the livestock leased, as well as homage and services and there was also a lower interest rate arrangement involving a special payment.

It was the custom to 'fosterage' the children by sending them away to live with another family of a higher rank. This ended when they came of marriageable age, 17 for boys, 14 for girls. Compensation was made for this temporary adoption.

Banquets were a part of the Celtic social life and they were held at all the great festivals as well as for weddings and funerals. It was the responsibility of the king to provide feasts for his people. The wealthy class drank imported Italian wine, whilst the lower classes drank 'cornia', beer made out of wheat and honey. Drinking was made from a common cup carried by a slave and they all drank heavily. There were open hearths upon which were cauldrons and spits. The bravest hero was allowed to take the best piece of meat, but if another claimed it they fought together for supremacy. They sat on the floor on skins or straw and used low tables.

The nobility controlled necessary imports, such as salt and tin. Skilled craftsmen, goldsmiths and blacksmiths, worked for them. The finer pottery was just for the aristocracy.

The majority of the early Celtic dwellings were constructed of wood, but between the 4th and 6th centuries BC humbler dwellings were stone-walled circular huts, with conical roofs covered with thatch. There was a central hearth for cooking and heating and a hole in the roof let out the smoke. Nearby grain would be grown and cattle raised.

By the 7th century BC the Celts knew the techniques of working with bronze and they could cast it into ornaments and tools, or produce it into sheets for making vessels, which they could decorate by beating out designs. Once the use of iron became known its extraction became widespread and it was used for tools and weapons, because of its greater strength. There was no shortage of copper or tin and gold, silver, coral, amber and glass were always available for the wealthy in the form of ornaments. Graphite and hemetite for pottery were also widely available.

In the late 3rd century BC the Celts of Central and Western Europe began adopting coinage for their own use. By the beginning of the 1st century BC coins had reached SE Britain.

Agriculture in the Iron Age

The wheat grown gave very high yields. Their fields, rectangular in shape, were usually between a quarter and a third acre and could be ploughed in a day, using a swing plough. The two main occupations of the Celts were cereal growing and stock rearing. The cereals they grew were einkorn, spelt and emmer and they could produce almost a tonne per acre with them. They also grew barley for beer making, rye, oats, millet and buckwheat. Out of the flour they made bread, girdle cakes or porridge. The grain stored in pits was for seed grain, or for trading with. The ears were usually stored without threshing and were only threshed when required.

Peas, lentils and beans were also grown and, in suitable areas, cabbages, carrots, turnips, garlic and onions. Many wild plants and berries, and apples and pears in the forests, were also used. Flax and hemp were grown. Woad was used for the blue dye to decorate themselves and madder root was used for red dye. The women painted their bodies blue when attending funerals.

Baskets were made from osiers and rushes. For tools they had hoes, shovels, rakes, sickles and scythes. Their swing plough was fitted with an iron share from the 5th century BC. Cattle were used for ploughing and were also a source of milk and meat. The cattle, a small short-horn variety (since disappeared), were the Celts' source of wealth. They had domesticated the pig, smaller than today's, and its meat was much favoured by the Celts, who also exported salted pork. They kept a small variety of sheep, from which they plucked the wool. Goats were kept for their milk. They also had hens, ducks and geese, as well as cats and dogs. On the coast, line and net fishing was practised and they also used shellfish.

There were blacksmiths, bronzesmiths and goldsmiths. Iron, in the form of ingots, was obtained from the production centres, and weighed between 11 and 13 lbs. Later the ingots were replaced by long flat bars, which were not only used to manufacture a large variety of articles, but were used as currency too. The bronzesmiths became very skilful and their products were highly decorated and ornamented, and they were able to fuse colours into the copper.

They seemed to have preferred to work in wood rather than in stone and to make wooden vessels rather than use ceramics.

Since the later Bronze Age in Europe, the horse has been extensively used by man. First leather then bronze fittings were used. Draught and riding horses were used, cavalry units became part of their warfare, as well as chariots horses.

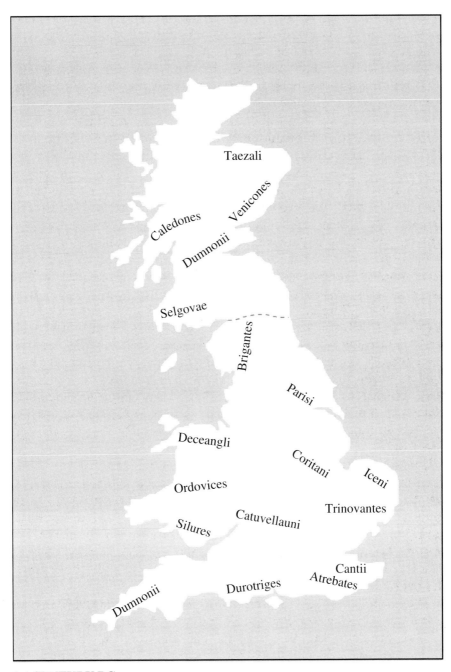

1st CENTURY BC

Throughout the Stone Age there was one standard of measurement (a yardstick), equal to about 83 centimetres, and it is more than likely that this continued into the period of the Celts.

The egg-shaped stone circles were constructed so as to fit into an internal design of triangles. The diameter of the circles was calculated to exact measurements.

The Druids used rods which they placed between the standing stones, or in holes forming an outer circle, in order to give them exact calculations in their 16 month a year calendar.

The Plough

At first the Celts used a light plough, called an ard, which just scratched a furrow in the earth. There were two kinds, the simple one called a 'crook ard', with the beam and sole made from one piece of wood. The other called a 'spade ard', had the stilt and share inserted through a hole in the separate beam. Iron shears were later used as well as iron shoes over the wooden tip. They were drawn by two oxen and guided by one ploughman. Vast areas of Europe were ploughed up by these two types of plough. It was necessary to plough an area twice, the second time at right angles to the first. Prior to the Roman conquest heavy ploughs had been invented using an iron knife and a wooden mould which turned over the earth and enabled heavy land to be ploughed for the first time. The field system began to appear.

The Wheel

At first cast bronze wheels were used. The spoked wooden wheel, mainly used for funerary carts, appeared in the 7th century BC, but the art of wheel making was not fully mastered until the 5th century BC, when shrunk-on iron tyres were used. When war chariots appeared in the 5th century BC a lighter but much stronger wheel was required. The felloe was formed from one piece of ash bent to shape. The wheels had turned elm hubs and turned willow spokes.

2

Principal Tribes

The *AEDUI*. The chief tribe in Central France, who placed themselves under Caesar's protection.

The *ARVERNI*. A powerful tribe in the Massif Central. They were anti-Roman.

The *BOII*. In the 5th century BC they made a large migration from north of the Alps to the Po Valley, Italy, the rest remaining in Bohemia, but were forced to migrate into France.

The *BRIGANTES*. So named after their Goddess Brigantia, meaning 'The High One'. They occupied the whole of Northern England.

The *DUROTRIGES*. Inhabited Dorset. The Romans had to destroy over 20 of their hillforts before they would capitulate.

The *ERAVISCI*. They occupied Hungary.

The *HELVETII*. They inhabited Switzerland. In the 1st century AD they migrated into Gaul. They had attempted to do so in 58 BC, but Caesar drove them back with a great loss of life to the Celts.

The *ICENI*. They occupied Suffolk and Norfolk. They were pro-Roman, but took part in Queen Boudicca's rebellion.

The *NERVII*. They lived in central Belgium. They resisted Caesar strongly and were almost annihilated.

The *PARISII*. Inhabited the Paris area of France and were also in Britain.

The *SCORDISCI*. They migrated into Greece but had to return. They settled between the Drava and Sava.

The *TRINOVANTES*. They inhabited eastern England. They became Roman allies.

The *VENETII*. They inhabited the coastal region of Armorica (Brittany). They were shipping traders with Britain. In 50 BC they rebelled against the Romans who defeated them in a sea battle. Many of them were executed or sold as slaves. They had a fleet of 200 sailing ships.

The *VOLCAE*. They lived in Central Europe, in Southern Gaul and Anatolia.

Migrations and Campaigns

Prosperity and thus overpopulation forced the Celts to make a series of migrations. Large migrations began about 400 BC from Europe to Italy, Greece and Anatolia and carried on to about 200 BC. In the mid 4th century BC they attacked the Illyrians in Yugoslavia. In 387 BC Celts from Gaul overran northern Italy, and settled south of the Po, and remained there until the early part of the 2nd century BC. Some settled at Milan, and in Lombardy and Sicily. In 387 BC they defeated the Romans at the battle of Allia and sacked Rome. In 335 BC Celts were received by Alexander the Great, when they were campaigning in the Carpathians.

By the beginning of the 3rd century BC they had attacked Macedonia and Thrace and in 279 BC were in Greece. They also crossed into Asia Minor. In 279 BC 300,000 Celts under Breunus invaded Greece and, in spite of strong resistance by the Greek army, they reached Delphi and rifled the shrine, carrying off huge quantities of treasure. A terrific thunderstorm and landside, and a sudden attack by the Greeks, demoralised the Celts and they hurriedly retreated, being constantly harried on their way back northwards, and Breunus committed suicide. The surviving forces split up, some to the Beograd region, others to Transdanubia and to Asia Minor. The latter consisting of 20,000 men, women and children, entered the services of two local rulers, the men becoming mercenaries, raiding and plundering the southern kingdoms. These raids lasted many years. However, in 285 BC the Celts were defeated by an army using elephants. The Celts withdrew to the north and settled in Galatia, Turkey, but soon began to raid the south again.

In the 230s BC the king of Pergamum led an army against the Celts and defeated them and they retreated once more to Galatia. In the battle of Magnesia in 189 BC Pergamum and Rome defeated the northern kingdom and the 40,000 Celts in Galatia were enslaved. (It was to these Celts that St Paul addressed his letter to the Galatians.) According to St Jerome the Galatians spoke a language similar to the Treveri in Hunsrück-Eifel.

The Cimbri and Teutones, Germanic tribes, appeared in northern Italy at the end of the 2nd century BC.

Celts who went into mercenary service in the Mediterranean area were paid one gold piece per head for a campaign.

Migrations to Spain were made by the Celtiberi (Osima), of Brittany.

In 113 BC the Cimbri, who it is thought originated from Jutland, appeared in the eastern Alps and defeated a Roman force. In 105 BC the Cimbri, together with the Teutones, defeated another Roman force in south Gaul. They parted and in 102 BC the Teutones were destroyed by a Roman army at Aix-en-Provence. The Cimbri made their way into the Po Valley, but at Vercelli they were annihilated by the Romans.

In 107 BC the Celts defeated a Roman army at Bordeaux.

After the destruction of Rome in 390 BC the Celts remained a threat for 50 years and it was not until about 332 BC, after several battles, that a treaty was concluded. However, in 295 BC they were defeated by the Romans. In 225 BC the final defeat of the Celts came at the battle of Telamon. The Celts who had settled in the Po Valley were defeated at Lake Como in 197 BC and at Bologna in 191 BC. The Romans drove them out and took over their settlements. The remaining Celts moved to north of the Alps and to Hungary and Czechoslovakia.

In 58 BC the Helvetii, of Switzerland, burned their villages and set out for new and larger territory in Gaul, only to be attacked by Caesar, who defeated them at Armecy and forced the *remnanta* to return to Switzerland. Of the 368,000 who set out, of whom 92,000 were men under arms, less than a third returned home.

By 82 BC the threat to Italy from the Celts had come to an end.

3

Gallia Belgica

The area of this country was from the Seine to the Rhine, and from the Channel to Switzerland.

From Kempen and Limburg in the north to Ardennes in the south are rich burials as well as urnfield ones. In Champagne they are usually flat graves with inhumation. In the Argonne creations were made. The Hunsrück-Eifel has an overlap between the two. Burgundy, Württemberg and the Jura have very rich burials. There was a wagon burial at Vix (6th century BC) where there was Attic pottery, Etruscan and Greek bronze and Greek gold. This burial is connected with the hillfort of Mount Lassois. A similar burial was at Henneburg.

Much trade was done through the Greek colony at Marseille, but this came to a sudden halt about 500 BC with the destruction of these hillforts and others in the Rhône, Lorraine and Jura. The Celts gave their names to Arras and Artois.

The La Tène culture influence can be found in the Alps, Bohemia and Rhineland. The Hunsrück-Eifel graves of chieftains contained much gold and a variety of imported goods. Basse-Yutz produced the finest of ornamented flagons. There were rich burials at Altrier, Weiskirchen and Schwarzenbach, with gold ornaments.

Some hillforts were inhabited while others were just used as refuges. There were numerous chariot burials, e.g. la Gorge-Meiller and Somme-Bionne. In the Ardennes burials have been made under stone cairns. There are rich burial sites in the hillfort of Kemmelberg in Flanders, Leval-Trahegnies in Hainant and Eigenbilzen in Limberg, as well as the Rhineland sites of Reinheim and Waldalgesheim.

The people who Caesar called 'Belgae' were of germanic origin, from the Danube between Bohemia and Carpathia. They arrived in the mid 3rd century BC period in two groups, the westerly one formed Belgium and the northerly the coastal area. Their cemeteries were quadrangular or circular. Their wealthier women wore ankle rings. A Gallic calendar from the 1st century BC, written on bronze plaques, was found at Coligny and covered a five-year period.

The Late Iron Age

In the 3rd century BC there was a drop in population in the Hunsrück-Eifel and Champagne areas, but there were settlements in the valley. (Belgios led a raid into Greece. Veridomarus was the leader of the Insubres in Italy.)

There is an important cemetery at Pernant (Aisne). Most burials were by cremation in the 2nd century BC, except in the Ardennes where it continued to be the tumulus burial. A few chariot burials occurred as at les Pothées in the Ardennes and torcs were found at Frasnes-lez-Buissenal, Tournai. In the 1st century BC one chariot burial has been found at Armentieres. A chariot burial was made near the small hillfort at Happstädten-Weutsbach. In ordinary graves pottery, spears, swords and glass ornaments have been found. While small settlements of a few families are still the norm, villages were founded at Horath and Wederath on the Hunsrück ridges.

Small Celtic fields were used in Kempen and larger ones in Picardie. A heavy plough was used in Rosmeer, Limberg. In northern Gaul iron ore was of great importance. In Champagne it was agriculture. The Romans called the Gauls *Gallia Comata*, shaggy-haired Gauls.

Hillforts

Farmsteads were usually surrounded by a ditch system making a double enclosure. At Conchel-le-Temple and Bundenbach were two rectangular houses, together with numerous post holes, suggesting a small settlement of one or two families. A very large structure, with post holes measuring $22\,m \times 12\,m$ has been found at Veriberie (Oise).

Agricultural settlements were at Kamps Veld, at Haps (Nijmegen) and Mechelen-Nekkerspoel. The rectangular four or six-post hut was widely used. Larger houses have been found at Mayen. The hillfort at Beaufort was a fortified farmhouse. There were small hillforts at Erden (Mosel) and Bundenbach (Hunsrück).

The latter were refortified in the 2nd century BC and destroyed about 100 BC. In the hillforts of Etival (Vosges) and Otzenhausen were iron workings.

Two types of rampart are known in the time of Caesar, the timber-laced ones and the massive dump ones, which were later developed. The hillfort at Vieux-Laon shows both construction styles. There were large fortifications at Tetelbierg and Donnersberg. Undefended centres of production were at Aulnat and Levroux. There were many hillforts in Lorraine and at Vieux-Chalons and Vieux-Reims. Hillforts at Vermand, Mt César, Tetelbierg, Otzenhausen and Donnersberg were built for their commanding position. The one at Tetelbierg is built on a hill containing iron ore. Gournay-sur-Aronde (Oise) was another site, while in the Meuse Valley were hillforts.

Coinage

Coins came into use between the mid-3rd and mid-2nd centuries BC. Tarentine gold coins of late 4th century BC were copied. They were used in Hunsrück and Saarland, mainly for doweries and gifts. They had a man-headed horse on the reverse and on the obverse the head of Apollo. In the Rhine area between Koblenz and Mainz a Pegasus reverse was used. In Lorraine a Janus head was used. The Somme Valley Staters used Apollo heads. A hoard of these were found at Tayac (Gironde) dated from before 100 BC. After being defeated by the Romans, the inhabitants to the east of the lower Rhone adopted silver coins copied from the Roman, with a helmeted head on the obverse. They became widely used and had a long life, first with a Greek name and later with a Roman one. Bronze coins were also later introduced.

Gaul

From 700–400 BC the leaders were immensely rich and received rich burials. They populated an area from Bohemia to Burgundy. The rich burials of the early period took place in Bohemia and Bavaria. The peasants had simple cremation graves. In the graves of warriors their swords were buried with them. Some were provided with a joint of pork or goose, and a knife, whilst some had vessels in pottery or bronze.

In the 6th century BC the rich burial zone moved to the area between Stuttgart and Zurich, the Jura and Burgundy. In the 5th century BC this zone moved to the Middle Rhine and Marne area. The two most important sites were Mont Lassois in the Seine valley and Heuneberg, Swabian Alb. Near Mont Lassois, at Vix, in 1953, a tomb of a 6th century BC woman, filled with rich objects (jewellery, bracelets, torcs, a necklace and golden diadem) was found. She was about 35 years old and dressed in her finery.

Under the Hochmichele mound, near Heuneburg, there was also a rich burial chamber of a woman with a funeral cart. 13 other burials were found in this mound.

In the 1st century BC in France hillforts were built to stem the Roman advance, also at this period urban centres developed all over Europe.

The Romans recorded that large amounts of gold and silver bullion were kept stored in lakes by the Celts. After the Roman conquest they sold lakes by public auction on that account.

At the source of the Seine the Celts erected a shrine. The Romans also built over it. On this site Napoleon III erected a grotto. In 1963 a number of wooden votives, in waterlogged condition were found here, mainly carved from oak, and included 27 complete human figures, heads, limbs and trunks. There were also 22 wooden plaques carved to represent human organs, bronze and stone votives of eyes, organs, heads, hands and feet, proving that this shrine was an important pilgrimage site.

In the Vendée area of France 32 votive shafts were discovered.

In Gaul the Romans instituted annual gatherings of representatives, called *Concilium Gallierum*. With the Romanisation of Gaul Celtic art died out.

Belgium

Belgium in Caesar's day was a wedge-shaped area from the coast between the Seine and Saume Valley to the Oise, Aisne and Marne and inhabited by the Ambiani, Bellovaci and Suessioes. Forests and rivers formed natural boundaries between the tribes. To the east and south-east of Belgium were the Remi tribe, who sided with Caesar.

The northern Belgae inhabited the area from Boulogne to the Meuse. The Atrebates occupied Artois and part of Flandre/

francais, and had the hillforts at Arras and Escant. Flanders was inhabited by the Menapii. The Nervii people occupied the land bounded by the Escant-Scheldt to the Hainant. They alone of all the Gaulish people had no cavalry and they built hedges to deter enemy horsemen. The Atuatuci were in northern Limburg and Kempen, and the Eburones were in the northern Eifel. The Treveri were on the SE edges of the Ardennes, Eifel and Hunsrück.

Normandy

There are Iron Age hillforts at Camp de Chatelier, Petit-Celland, and at Chateux Gontier, Courbe, and Iron Age camps at Camp de Bierre, Mevri, Cité des Limes, Bracquemont, Camp du Cotelieur, Duclair, Camp du Canada, Fécamp, Camp de César, Sandouville.

4

The Roman Conquest

When the Aedui, friends of the Romans, were threatened by the Helvetii, Caesar took the opportunity to wage war on them, and defeated them. Caesar also took the opportunity to proceed against the incomer Ariovistus, and after defeating him, stationed six legions in winter quarters at Besançon.

In the following Spring of 57 BC the Belgae tribes reacted against the Roman presence and gathered forces against him. As both the Lingones and Remi declared themselves friendly Caesar was allowed free passage through their territory and increased his forces to eight legions. A large Belgic force had gathered under the king of the Suessiones, Galba. The Roman army crossed the Aisne, north of Reims, and encamped there. The Belgae marched SE and attacked the Romans but without success and were forced to retreat, pursued by the Romans, to whom they surrendered. The leaders of the Belgae fled to Britain.

Caesar continued his march NE to attack another force of Atrebates, Veromandui and Nervii. The force retreated before the Roman army and finally surrendered. A further force of Atuatuci concentrated on a fort, but when the Roman army arrived, they too surrendered, but later attacked the Romans. As a reprisal Caesar is said to have sold 50,000 of them into slavery, a crushing blow to the Belgae.

Satisfied by his campaign Caesar took up winter quarters in the lower Loire, which indicated that a campaign against Britain might be undertaken. This resulted in a revolt by the Armoricans (in Brittany), which kept Caesar busy suppressing them during 56 BC. In the late summer he led a campaign against the Morini and Menapii, but they withdrew into the marshes and forests. He resumed his campaign against them in 55 BC, as he needed their ports for a British invasion. However, an invasion by tribes who crossed the Rhine, forced Caesar to make an expedition into Germany, where he defeated the enemy and constructed a bridge over the Rhine, which he destroyed before returning to the coast and proceeded with his expedition against Britain, taking some of the nobility with him. During his absence some of the Morini revolted and were only subdued after reprisals.

It is thought Caesar disembarked from the ports of Wissant and Sangatte. Roman bases were at Bretenil, Folleville and Vendeil-Caply. (The hoard at Frasnes-ley-Buissenal containing gold torcs and coins could have been made during this war period.) The Romans raised military units from the local inhabitants and paid them with silver coinage.

The Treveri were always a source of danger to the Romans, due to their well-trained cavalry, their closeness to the Rhine and their unreliability. Caesar decided to make them submit and proceeded to march against them. The Treveri retreated into the security of the forests but eventually surrendered.

Caesar had difficulty in providing provisions for his army. In 54 BC a drought caused a poor harvest, so that for winter quarters it was necessary to split up the army. Caesar himself lodged in Amiens.

The Eburones declared war on the Romans in Atuatuca, and lured them out into an ambush from which only a few Romans survived. Whereupon the triumphant tribesmen lay siege upon the Roman camp of Cicero. Here they used siege towers and heated sling balls but the Romans managed to keep them at bay until Caesar arrived with two legions who routed the Gauls. When Caesar attacked the hillfort of the Atuataci, in the Meuse region, he captured the whole population of 53,000 and auctioned them all in one lot.

The last two Celtic leaders to oppose Caesar were Ambiorix, Chief of the Ebarones, who led the Belgic revolt in 54/53 BC. He escaped, but the Romans destroyed every village and building, slaughtered all the animals and confiscated the food stocks, so that what people were left were left to starve. The other leader was Vercingetorix, who led a revolt the following year, but also failed, and his force was defeated. This left Caesar in control of Gaul, although further revolts were to follow. Caesar in his attack against Vercingatorix and his forces, destroyed one stronghold after another. After a long and bitter siege at Avaricum the stronghold fell, and out of 40,000 inhabitants only 800 escaped. The rest were slaughtered without mercy by the Romans. The Romans then moved on to engage Vercingatorix and his forces, who had taken up position at the foot of the stronghold of Girgovia. Here the Romans suffered a defeat, and retired to rebuild their forces. Later a cavalry engagement took place at which the Gauls were routed. This was a great blow to Vercingatorix, who moved to the hillfort at Alesia, having sent for a relieving force. Meanwhile Caesar had arrived and surrounded the fort with strong fortifications. When the expected Gauls arrived, a force of a quarter of a million men, they were unable to penetrate the Roman defences, and in a final encounter the Gauls were defeated (in 52 BC), and Vercingatorix and his forces had to surrender. He was held prisoner for six years, paraded through Rome and then strangled. (In 1865 Napoleon III erected a statue of him at Alesia.)

Thus after eight years of war and revolt the Gauls had finally to accept defeat. This was due to Caesar's brilliant war strategy and tactics and to his often ruthless and savage treatment of the defeated enemy. This was the end of Celtic supremacy in Europe.

However, unrest continued amongst the tribes and Caesar was forced to continue his campaign against them, but with an extra three legions, and successfully drove the Treveri across the Rhine. A second bridge was built. Caesar now split up his forces but nothing was accomplished and he had to content himself by laying waste the land.

He and his army took much booty during his campaign. When he came to Gaul he was heavily in debt, but when he left he had so much gold the price of it fell in Italy.

After the ending of Caesar's campaigns in Gaul, Rome had little interest in the country. Roman colonies had been formed at Lyon, Augot and Nyon and the first roads were constructed from Lyon to the Rhine and Channel coast.

Caesar divided Gaul into four provinces, Narbonensis, Aquitania, Lugdunensis and Belgica. These were sub-divided into *civitates*, which were about the same as the old tribal areas. He imposed on Gaul a tribute of 40 million sesterces, to be paid annually.

The presence of the Roman army in Gaul led to importations from Italy of pottery, which local people copied.

Augustus decided to create a province Germania in 12 BC and a great altar was set up at Cologne. At the end of Augusta's reign schools had been established to transform the sons of Gaulish nobility into Romanised citizens. Large areas of Gaul attained Latin status in the 1st century AD.

For a Gaul to be chosen as a delegate was a great honour, but to be chosen as High Priest for a year was the greatest honour it was possible to receive.

Belgica was governed by a legate of praetorian rank, who resided in Reims, and he had total responsibility. Non-Romans had no right of appeal against his judgements. The procurator of Belgica was also Paymaster of the Rhine armies.

A serious revolt against the Romans occurred in 69–70 AD, but the Gauls were defeated at Besançon and land was confiscated. However, the revolt continued and there was a massacre at Metz. The final battle was at Trier where the Gauls put up a good fight but were defeated. Honourable terms were negotiated, but the bid for independence had failed.

Belgic Gauls in the 2nd century AD had the option of taking service in the Roman army, but as this usually meant service overseas, it was not very popular.

Palladius, a 5th century Gaulish writer, mentioned the invention of a reaping machine. Wheeled ploughs were also in use.

The use of bread wheat increased and rivalled spelt. Emmer and einkorn declined. Rye increased but barley declined. Buckwheat went out of use.

Carrots, parsnips, beets, turnips, cabbage, lettuce and celery were grown. Garlic, coriander and dill were imported. Walnuts and chestnuts were native. Flax was extensively cultivated.

Sheepfarming was important, and Belgic woollen garments were exported to Italy, and well known for their good quality.

Good quality iron ore could be found at Entre-Sambre-et-Meuse, the Ardennes, southern Belgium, Luxembourg and Lorraine. Lead was very scarce in Belgica, although it was mined at St Avoid. It was probably imported from Britain as well as tin. Copper and zinc were mined in the Saarland-Eifel and Eifel-Ardennes areas.

Salt was exploited, especially in the Lorraine and in the Seille Valley. Also coastal regions at Zeebrugge, Raversijde and Ardres were sites of salt production. Wood was the main source of fuel.

Pottery was manufactured at Lyon and southern Gaul and exported. It was mainly in black or red colour. At Boucheporn-Moselle were 30 kilns and 60 potteries.

Wine was imported from Italy and olive oil and fish sauce from Spain.

The road network was Langres–Trier–Cologne in the east, Langres–Reims–Amiens–Boulogne in the west and Amiens–Bavay–Cologne in the north.

5

Armorica (Brittany)

In the gallery grave of Penker, Finistère, were found, besides Late Neolithic items, a beaker, a long copper dagger, an archer's wrist guard and a bone button with V perforation. Thirteen wrist guards have been found in Brittany. Two solid gold bracelets were found at the foot of a menhir at Saint Cado. A bracelet, two copper axes, a gold ring and fragments of a ribbon torc were found in a Passage Grave at Saint-Père-en-Retz. Objects of precious metal have only been found along the coastline. At Trentemoult a javelin head and nine flat copper axes were found. Some Passage graves were re-used in the Iron Age and Gallo-Roman period. The cemetery at Lesconil, Finistère, was used up to the Bronze Age and in a Passage grave were two flange axes, one flat chisel shaped axe, and eight amber space plates. Bronze or gold hoards have been found near the foot of menhirs.

Bronze Age barrows were excavated in 1843 at Lothéa, Quimperlé and Finistère and in 1865 at Tanwedon. There is a large concentration along the Blavet and southern edge of the Monts d'Arrée. In some of the barrows in the Trégor area they appear to have been roofed in by wooden beams and the grave goods in wooden boxes. Between 200 to 250 barrows are probably of the Bronze Age period. The number of known hoards found amount to 382.

Finistère	140
Côtes-du-Nord	102
Morbihan	65
Ille-et-Vilaine	39
Loire-Atlantique	36

About 188 had socketed axes. A total of 20,000 implements were found.

In the Middle Bronze Age hoards became larger. The flanged axe appeared later to be supplanted by the palstave. The sword with a broad base and hollow hilt, also appears. A large hoard was found at Tréboul. The axe of the Middle Bronze Age was narrow. 360 were found at Calorguen, some being decorated. Spear heads of this period were with fairly broad barbs. Heavy bracelets of solid metal have been found, with some decoration.

In the Late Bronze Age razors, socketed hammers and gouges appear, as well as knives, chisels, nails, buttons and belt plaques. Of the Middle Bronze Age about 1,800 palstaves have been found. Between the Bronze Age and Iron Age the metal industry was in full production. Some axe heads were decorated and some had quadrangular sockets. Socketed axes are the most prolific in the northern areas. Mauche had 74 hoards, with a total of 8,500 axes.

Ille-et-Vilaene	18 hoards with 5,500 axes
Côtes-du-Nord	69 hoards with 6,100 axes
Finistère	72 hoards with 7,100 axes
Morbihan	23 hoards with 1,700 axes
Loire-Atlantique	6 hoards with 89 axes

More Bronze Age gold objects have been found in Brittany than anywhere else in France. In an Early Bronze Age treasure trove at Kerivoa was a lunula, two small ones, a head band, and two pieces of wire torcs. At Maël-Pestivieu was a gold ring-disc and two bronze ingots. Lunlae and spiral torcs were imported from Ireland in the Early Bronze Age. After the Middle Bronze Age torcs in various forms are found twisted in spirals, some massive. Round or flat bracelets have been found, as well as necklaces and coiled ear rings. Bracelets probably came from Galicia and Ireland.

At Questembert fragments of wattle from the walls of a dwelling house were found, also a jar filled with roasted acorns, and pieces of a quern. At Plomeur was the site of a dwelling, used from the Neolithic to the Iron Age. A Bronze Age knife, a spear head and a bronze pin were found. At Ploubaylance was a fortified Bronze Age settlement.

Metal workers used clay and wood moulds, but at the end of the Bronze Age, bronze moulds were common. Cakes of copper have been found. At Huelgoat silver, lead and copper was found.

An iron sword was found in the Douges marshes and another in the Goulaine marshes. In barrows at Le Rocher were bracelets of iron and bronze, and in a tomb were 24 bronze and two iron bracelets. Also found were rings, nails, fragments of weapons and blue glass beads. A small barrow at the Gree de Carate has been carbon dated to 450 plus/minus 60 BC.

A huge cemetery is at Saint Urnel where hundreds of bodies were buried, dating from the 1st to 2nd centuries Iron Age to the beginning of the Roman occupation. At Rennes a cast bronze belt clasp of Italian make was found. At Tronran parts of an iron helmet were found. The finest interior hillfort is at Kercaradec.

The oldest Etruscan object found in Armorica in the tumulus du Rocher at Le Bono was a bronze vessel 6th/7th century BC, bronze bracelets were also found. A gold coin from Cyrene, struck between 322 and 315 BC was found at Finistère. A beautiful engraved pot was found in a tumulus at Kernevey, Saint Pol-de-Leon, Finistère. A 5th century BC cremation urn was found at Lana-Tinikei, Plomeur, Morbihan. There are several hundred Iron Age stones with markings. One six foot stone at Sainte-Anne-en-Tregastel is marked with interlaced S's. A 5th century ceramic engraved bowl was found in a cave at Plouegat-Moysau, Finistère. A carved pyramid-shaped granite stone of 4th century BC was found at Kerinaria-en-Pont L'Abbé, Finistère and another seven foot high carved conical standing stone was at Kervadel, Ploban-nalec, Finistère.

In the Iron Age the area around Pointe du Ray, Finistère, was heavily populated. Six fortified headlands have been found there.

In Armorica 36,000 axes were buried in over 250 hoards. In the bay of Douarneuey, Finistère, at Plomarc'h Pella, are remains of considerable salt workings, where sardines and tunny fish were prepared. Other sites were at Lorient and in the bay of Saint-Brienc.

There are many Iron Age hillfort and camp sites. Pointe de Vieux Chateau, Sanzon, is a hillfort site, also Castel Finans, St Aignan, Camp de César, Ile-de-Groix, Castennec Bieenzig, Lostmarc'h, Croyon, Castel Pen-Lédon, Folgoët, Camp d'Artas, Huelgoat, Castel Mear was a promontory fort, also Menei-Castel, Pont Croix, and Toul Goielic. Camps were at Chateau des Anglais, Cambremer, Beg-eu-Aud, Auray, Pointe de Meinga, St Malo, Coz-Yaudet, and Camp de Péran. Other hillforts were at Cap D'Erquy and at Castel Coz. Bayeux was the site of an Iron Age settlement of the Baiocasses tribe. Lisieux was the centre of the Lexovic tribe. At Le Rocher is an inhumation burial site where

24 bronze and two iron bracelets were found. The Coriosolites gave their name to Corseul, and the Veneti to Vaunes. 14,000 coins were found under the floor of a villa at Moné-Vécheun, Ploninec. Vannes and Rennes were fortified between 275 and 300 AD. At Lochronan annual gatherings took place round a large boulder.

In the Iron Age peoples arrived speaking the Celtic language and giving Celtic names to many places, and they seem to have settled in a land already populated.

Armorica had a busy maritime community, trading for tin from the Britons, and possessing a large fleet of sea going vessels, and they were expert navigators.

Their ships, of which they had about 200, were square rigged, with leather sails, and with a rudder on the port side aft. They were about 100 feet long and had a beam of nearly 30 feet.

The main cross Channel port in Britain was Hengistbury Head. Later Colchester took over this trade.

There had already been contacts with S Wales for a long time and Cornwall had traded in tin. The new territory of the migrants was divided up into three kingdoms, Dumnonia, Bro Erech and Cornouaille.

The second quarter of the 5th century AD saw the beginning of the emigration of the Britons from Cornwall and south and east Wales to western Armorica, due to the pressure of Irish raiders and settlers and it continued to the beginning of the 7th century. By the end of the 6th century the land was called *Britannia*.

For several centuries Armorica produced good quality ceramic articles.

Brittany became part of France in 1532.

6

Germany

Manching, in Upper Bavaria, was an industrial settlement, with ramparts 7 km in length, enclosing an area of 700 acres, laid out in streets of wooden buildings. Iron working was carried out from nearby deposits of bog iron. Copper and bronze were also worked for brooches and cart fittings, from stone moulds. Coins were minted. Glass beads, bracelets and high class pottery were made. Weaving was also done.

The ramparts were solidly constructed of stone and timber, called by the Romans *murus Gallicus*.

It was the chief town of the Vendelici, and was inhabited during the 1st century BC and then suffered destruction.

At Holzhausen, in Bavaria, a rectangular ritual enclosure was built surrounded by a palisade. Three votive shafts were sunk, the deepest being 40 metres. There are two flat inhumation cemeteries at Steinbichel and Hundsrücken. Another square cult site with deep shafts is at Tomerdingen, south Germany. In Bavaria they were common in isolated areas of woodland. The largest burial ground in Europe was constructed at Magdalenenberg, near Villingen, Black Forest. Long iron swords were found at Mindelheim, Bavaria. The most excavated site is the Henneberg hillfort, Baden-Württemberg. During the 6th and 5th centuries BC it was rebuilt several times. At Wasserburg in Buchau there was a marsh fort. Graphite clays for pottery were produced at Passau and exported to Manching. Graphite paint was also used. At Leubingen in East Germany was a timber chamber under a barrow. There were wagon burials, as at Hart-an-der-Alz, Bavaria, where there was a collection of bronze vessels.

There was a change in bronze swords, due to larger castings. They became flange hilted and known as Hemingkofen and Erbenheim. They began as short daggers, then they were made larger, and finally to a rapier and then the true sword, with flange hilt and wooden handle. They were widely distributed.

Manching pottery

From Manching

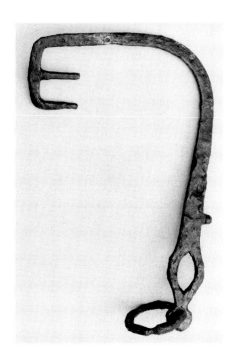

From Manching

From Manching

32

From Manching

In the German Mittelgebirge, Hesse, Thuringen, north Bavaria and Bohemia, many hillforts were established in the 5th century BC. By the 1st century BC many of these sites were important industrial and trading centres. At Gross Romstedt in Thuringia is an all male cemetery, end of 1st century BC to early AD.

Austria

On the mountain, Magdalensberg (3470 ft), near Willersdorf, Klagenfurt, Carinthia, was an ancient Celtic settlement sited on the southern slope, where this area was abundantly supplied with water, and was very fertile. It was also well suited for defence and was surrounded by defence works.

It was a metal manufacturing town, with blacksmiths and brass-founders, who used iron, copper and zinc, made steel and brass articles and minted silver coins. Also they made anvils, rings, hooks, iron vessels and high quality iron swords, made of iron strips welded together were produced. (Pliny wrote that these swords were only rivalled by those made by the Parthians and Chinese.)

It was founded about 300 BC and was part of the Celtic kingdom of Noric, and had between 3,000 and 5,000 inhabitants. It largely traded with Italy, and Italian traders settled there in 100 BC and its people were pro-Roman.

When the Romans arrived in 15 BC and occupied that area, they left the Celtic town undisturbed, and built their own town at the foot of the mountain in 45 AD, and called it *Claudium Virunum*, and it became the seat of government of the new Roman province. The Romans built an official quarter for their representative in the Celtic town, and by 45 AD the Norici had become largely Romanised. In their town was a building used for the assembly of the leaders of the Noric tribes.

In 15 BC the king of Norica died and bequeathed his kingdom to the Roman people. By 14 BC the Rhine–Danube frontier had been accomplished by the Romans.

The first excavations of the site began in 1948. In the cellars of the Italian traders dwellings were found hundreds of trading accounts scratched on the walls. One went to Mauratania in North Africa. There is a temple and Roman bath, and metal workers manufactury buildings, apart from their living quarters.

A museum has been built there to house the many Celtic artefacts.

Burials at Klein Klein produced swords, bronze helmets, a bronze cuirass and bronze vessels. Graphite clays for pottery were exported to Hallstatt from Passau.

Switzerland

There were hillforts at Wittnauer Horn and Burgenrain, and cemeteries at Münsingen, near Berne, and at St Sulpice. The former is the most famous Iron Age cemetery after Hallstatt. It was used from about 450 BC to 100 BC.

In 1962 near Erstfeld, Canton Uri, under a boulder on a pass, were found five gold bracelets and two torcs.

Spain

It is thought the Celts came to Spain in two waves between the 6th and 4th centuries BC, coming from Europe via the Pyrenees. They met with great resistance in some regions from old established tribes, but in other places they were able to settle without resistance. These earlier inhabitants were known as Iberians, so named by the Greek, Scylax, in the 6th century BC. These peoples inhabited the regions near to the Pyrenees, the eastern Mediterranean zone and part of the South. Galicia, and almost the whole of Portugal was dominated by the Celts. The rest of the country was occupied by the mixed tribes, who were given the name of Celtiberians, whose principal territory was known as Celtiberia, which included part of Castille and Aragon. The Celts used a dagger known as *herradura* (horseshoe). The most important city of the Celtiberians was Numantia, which was captured by invaders in 133 BC. Excavations at Numantia have revealed streets with houses and cellars, arms, and a variety of decorative pottery with geometrical designs. Of the tribes at that time were the Gaelaeci, the Astures, the Cantabri, the Vascones, the Cerretani, the Turduli, the Lusitani, the Celtiberians, the Vaccaei, the Vettones, the Carpetani and the Ovetani.

Most of them lived in unfortified little villages, or scattered over the fields, but some in towns. Towers or fortified places were common to several villages, and at times corresponded to the capital of the tribe.

Marriage was generally monogamous, although there was polygamy. The family head was usually the father, but sometimes was the mother. However, the family was not the chief social unit, but the *gentilitas*, which was a group of families, inter-related or from a common stock. They were ruled by an assembly, or chief, with authority over the *gentilitas*. Each of these had their own Gods, and lived in one village which had a name. They had slaves. A number of *gentilitates* formed a tribe, which was ruled over by a king or an assembly. There were freemen, who were the wealthiest and strongest. In some tribes there was private property, in others it was communal ownership, when there was common working in the fields and common division of crops. Some tribes practised moon worship and some held sacrifices, both animal and human. Their principal food was meat, acorn bread, butter and a home-brewed drink. They were well dressed and had bronze helmets.

According to Strabo they were hardy, heroic, loved liberty, lacked discipline and loyal to the point of sacrifice. Their courage and military prowess meant they were much sought after as mercenaries and they saw service in Sicily, Africa, Greece and Italy. Votive offerings have been found in sanctuaries. When the Romans invaded Spain in 218 BC some tribes were pro-Roman, but the Celts of the centre, north and west put up a stubborn resistance, which lasted over a long period. It was not until the beginning of the 1st century AD that the Romans finally conquered Spain. Where there was great resistance to them the Romans adopted very harsh and cruel measures, exiling whole sections of the population, destroying towns and their inhabitants and mutilating young men and selling them into slavery. Where they were well received they made treaties of alliance, and allowed the tribes to keep their independence. By the end of the 1st century AD a large part of Spain's population had become Romanised, but the Centre and North remained antagonistic to Roman culture and maintained their language and culture for a much longer

Spanish shield

From Spain

37

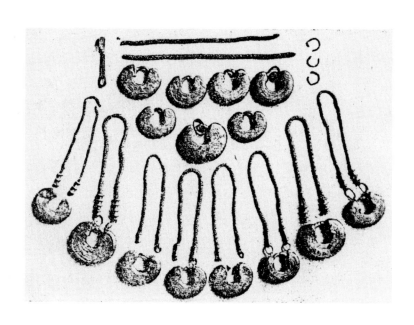

From Spain

38

From Spain

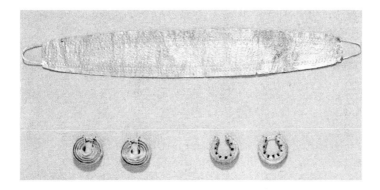

period especially in the rural areas. The Romans called Galicia *Gallaecia.*

Roman law caused the disappearance of the *gentiltates* and collective ownership and made Latin the national language. There was an impetus in mining, salting of fish, agriculture and sheep farming. A road system was developed, bridges were built and aqueducts constructed and many schools were founded. The Celts continued to make what they needed and left their art on tombs and statues found in Galicia and Portugal, with bronze idols and statues of bulls, boars, pigs and horses.

In Spain

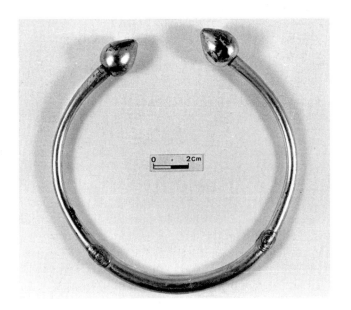

From Spain

40

From Spain

After the conquest was complete Christianity took birth, brought it is believed by St Paul and his disciples and by the 2nd and 3rd centuries there were numerous Christian communities, which suffered persecution from the Roman Emperors. Religious peace came at the beginning of the 4th century, and soon after the

From Spain

Christian Church became the official religion and was protected by the state, even so, the ancient religion of the Celts persisted in many places, especially in Galicia, where it was practised by Priscilian and his followers and it continued until the 6th century.

In 409 the Suevi, Vandals and Alani invaded Spain and wrestled

From Spain

the greater part of Galicia from Roman rule. In 585 the Visigoths came and destroyed the kingdom of the Suevi in Galicia.

A small settlement, and Celtic church and monastery, were established in Galicia by the Teutonic tribe of the Severi. It survived the raid of the Visigoths in 585 and retained its independence. The Celtic monastery of Santa Maria de Bretona, near Mondonhede, was included in the episcopate of Britonia. The first bishop was Mailoc. In the 5th century AD a city in Galicia was called Brigantia.

The Celtiberians of Western Spain were well known for their horsemanship and were employed by the Romans as auxiliaries.

St Fructuosus (early 7th century) founded island monastic retreats off the Galician coast and on the island of Cadic in Baetica. There were also many anchorite hermits.

Galicia has its own language *o galego*, said to be similar to Portuguese, and its own national dress, and its folk groups use bagpipes, *gaita galega*. Since the Middle Ages millions of pilgrims have visited Galicia.

Galicia

The 'Castros' were the fortified Celtic settlements, of which nearly 5,000 of them have been catalogued. They are generally found on small hills and are round or oval shaped. In some are still the stone walls of the dwelling houses.

A great collection of gold jewellery found in the Castros are housed in the most important Galician archaeological museums.

The Greeks called Galicia *Ofiusa* and the Greek geographer Estrabon, born 65 BC, gave a very detailed description of the land. He described the warriors as using small round shields, drinking beer, curing hams and dancing to the flute and bugle.

The mythical hero of the Galicians, King Breogán, is said to have used the site of Coruna for disembarking his armies. A 2nd century AD Roman stone-built lighthouse still stands here. It was built by Caius Sevius Lupus and called the Tower of Hercules. It stands 104 metres high and the light shines for 40 miles. It was restored in 1682 and again in 1788/90.

After the fall of the Roman Empire, the Swabians established an independent kingdom in Galicia and the new culture reached its peak in the 11th/12th centuries. The administrative, territorial and religious organisations were ahead in time and perfection of any other European nation and some organisations have lasted until present times, as well as people's names and the Galician language.

A pilgrimage route to Santiago grew up and temples, monasteries, sanctuaries, inns and hospitals grew along this route and a most beautiful basilica of Romanesque style was built at the end of it, at Compostela, 1075–1122. This route also opened up trade and brought art and culture too.

St Fructuoso, born in the Bierzo, in the old kingdom of Galicia, was one of the founders of monasticism at the beginning of the 7th century. The reformation came in the 11th and 12th centuries, when the greatest splendour of Galician culture appeared. The monasteries became the most important centres of colonising and cultural and religious activity. The greatest of these are at Sobrado, Oseira and Samos.

The oldest literary texts written in Galician language date from the end of the 12th century, and appear in the *Cancioneiros de Ajuda, Biblioteca Vaticana* and *Biblioteca Nacional* of Lisbon. The maturity of the language as early as the 12th century indicates a much earlier written or oral literary use. During the 12th and 13th centuries it became the cultural language of the north-east, and was kept as a literary language and used for the most important collection of poems of medieval lyrics.

When the kingdoms of Galicia and León were incorporated into Castile, the Galician language suffered and became only used orally.

In the middle of the 19th century, an enthusiastic revivalist movement, *Rexurdimento*, appeared, to use Galician as a literary and cultural language again. In 1906 the Galician Royal Academy was founded, which resulted in the formation of the *Irmandade dos amigos da Fala*, Brotherhood of Friends of the Language, and the founding of the magazine *NOS*. The number of publications in Galician has increased and so has the number of readers. The learning of the language is compulsory at all levels of teaching. It is also beginning to be used in some newspapers, and other means of social communication, and officially the Galician language is now on an equal footing with the Spanish language. The Galician language has given leading figures of universal literature like Rosalia de Castro, Curros Enriquez, Castelao, and Anxel Fole.

The Galician Flag, white with a blue diagonal stripe, was first hoisted in 1558. The Galician Emblem, seven crosses surrounding a goblet was first engraved by Albrecht Dürer. The seven crosses refer to the seven provinces of Galicia, and the goblet refers to the privilege of the Cathedral of Lugo to keep the Holy Sacrament continually exposed.

The Galician National Anthem was first performed in 1907, composed by Pascual Veiga, to the words of Eduardo Pondal. The March of the ancient Kingdom of Galicia dates from the Napoleonic period. The bagpipe is seen in romanesque sculptures. Galicia was considered the leader of the musical movement of all Europe in the 12th century. Today there are a great number of bands, choirs and dance groups. Galicia is a land of museums, in towns, villages and private houses. It is a land of peasants and cattle breeders. Its people are basically serious, honest, hardworking and hospitable with a love for festivals.

St James the Apostle after his missionary journey through Spain, returned to Jerusalem where in AD 44 he was beheaded by the Romans. His body was taken back to Galicia where it was buried. Eight centuries later his tomb was discovered. St James was then pronounced the protector of Spain, a church was built over the site of the tomb and a monastery nearby. This place later grew into the town of Santiago (St James) and it became a very important pilgrim town. The present cathedral is the third on this site.

The cockleshell was the emblem of the pilgrims and this can be seen in cathedrals and churches.

St James's Day is the 25th July and it is celebrated as the Galician National Day.

All over Galicia are stone crosses similar to those in Brittany.

In the village of El Cebrero are some early peasant cottages, built of stone in a circular shape, with low walls and conical thatched roofs. They are called *pallozas*, and are similar to the Iron Age dwellings. As the windows are only tiny it is very dark inside, and they had a central hearth, as there was no chimney. The people who still occupy these dwellings receive a government grant, as they are now historical monuments.

Many of the Galicians are fair haired with blue eyes, and short and stocky. Many farmers still use oxen and horses. Since 1978 Galicia has had pre-autonomous status and a president.

America and South America has received many Galician emigrants. Galicia has a population of about 2½ million.

Some Galicians attended, for the first time, the Celtic Festival, held in Scotland in July 1988.

Portugal

The NW corner of Portugal is called Costa Verde, originally Portucale, and covers over 3,000 sq. miles, and is known as the cradle of the Portuguese nation, originally inhabited by Celtic tribes. The market town of Barcelos gave Portugal its national symbol – the cockerel. In the Costa Verde there is a three-day religious festival in August, which attracts a great many pilgrims.

Further south, the Costa de Prata was also inhabited by the Celts. It is full of shrines, castles, monasteries and museums.

The south of Portugal is called the Algarve, and at Murça the pig was worshipped in ancient times. There is an Iron Age granite statue of a sow. It is the only place in Portugal to have retained its own dialect.

7

The Channel Islands

The Islands were well populated by Neolithic man, who lived in caves, and hunted the mammoth, woolly rhinoceros, reindeer, bison, horse, cave bear and brown bear.

Only one gold torc has been found, from St Helier, and this was probably of Irish origin. A few four-handled pots from Brittany have been found, two on Jersey at Mainlands and Bel Royal. The finest hoard was in Alderney at Longy Common (now in the Candie Museum, St Peter Port, Guernsey). It contained tools, lumps of metal and finished objects.

At the Huguettes, Longis Bay, Alderney, much pottery was made. One iron razor was found here. Graphite ware was imported to Jersey from Brittany.

Salt was produced at le Crocq, Rocquaene and Catarec on Guernsey, Beleroute Bay on Jersey, and on Herm. Small promontory sites were provided with defence works. St Peter Port, Guernsey became important. 31 warrior graves have been found, mainly on the west side of Guernsey, but one was found at St Peter Port. Some had swords, spear heads and shields.

During the period of the Roman Conquest contact was made with the Coriosolites in NE Brittany, and with the Cotentin tribe. Much of the Coriosolites' mint was brought to Jersey from Armorica and buried here. Four large hoards were found at le Catel de Royal, St Martin, and another at la Marquanderie, St Brelade, where 12,000 coins were found. Of the other hoards one was of 900 coins, and another 700 coins.

In the 1st century BC the Coriosolites built a small settlement of round huts at Tranquesons, St Saviour, Guernsey.

The Romans did not occupy the Channel Islands until the end of their British occupation, when they built a small fort at the Nunnery site on Alderney.

In 1787 the Governor of Jersey was presented with the passage grave at Mont de la Ville, and he had it removed to Henley-on-Thames and re-erected there.

It is recorded by Holinshed in 1587 regarding a megalithic grave on Alderney – 'a priest not long since did find a coffin of stone in which to lay the bodie of a huge giant whose fore teeth were so big as a man's fist.'

Alderney

A great many sites were destroyed when 13 forts were built in the 1850s and by the German army in the last war. A museum is at the Huret, St Annes, in the old school, and it houses a collection of finds on the island.

Guernsey

At the Jerbourg peninsular there are Iron Age (600 BC) earthworks. There is a triple line of banks and ditches about 165 metres long, on the site of earlier defences. The site at Tranquesons, St Saviour, of 15 defended huts, was probably a Coriosolites' settlement.

The Guernsey museum is at St Peter Port, and it has many prehistoric finds in it.

Jersey

At Grouville is an Archaeological museum containing Palaeolithic to Medieval material.

The original St Lawrence's church was 7th century. At Le Câtel de Royal, is a large Iron Age promontory fort defended by a high earthwork, now 200 metres long, 6 metres high and with a 9 metre base. At Le Pinacle, St Ouen, is a site used from the Neolithic to the Roman period. There was some Late Bronze Age pottery, a bronze ring and spear head, also Iron Age pottery with an Armorican coin AD 180–91.

The first Christian communities were founded by Celtic missionaries from western Britain. St Samson went to Guernsey and Branwalader of Brittany to Jersey. There were monastic settlements.

48

Britannia (derived from the Pretani tribe)

Before the Romans invaded Britain the country was already divided up into a great many Celtic kingdoms, each with its own king. In the north of Scotland were the Picts, the Dumnonii in the SW and the Votadiui in the SE. The north of England was occupied by the Brigantes, the largest and most powerful tribe, East Yorkshire by the Parisii, East Anglia by the Iceni, the Midlands by the Coritani, the Welsh Border by the Cornovii, Wales by the Ordovices, South Wales by the Demetae and Silures.

By 700 BC large migrations of Celts from France and the Low Countries had taken place and by the early part of the 5th century BC stronger migrations took place. In 600 BC Celts were in the NE of Scotland. In 250 BC Celts from Switzerland settled in the east and south coastal areas. They introduced the two wheel war chariot drawn by two ponies. In 500–450 BC Celts from France and the Low Countries migrated to the south coastal areas. Britain was then known as Albion. In the 2nd century BC Celts from Brittany migrated to Cornwall and then to the Cotswolds. In the late 2nd century BC Celts from Champagne settled in East Yorkshire, and in 100 BC people from Belgium, known as Belgae, settled in the London area, and traded with Rome. They brought the wheeled plough with them. They brought a higher standard of living with them. The Belgae introduced the first coinage into Britain, based on the coinage of their own Belgic Gaul, with whom they kept a trade relationship.

Brigantia

The north of England was occupied by the Brigantes, the most numerous and powerful of the forty tribes. The Hiberno-Celts came from Ireland via Scotland and Mona (Isle of Man) and settled on the high fell sides of north Cumberland. Their area began with Carrock and terminated at Culgaith ('the end of the garden'). Blencow was its most important settlement. They founded Carlisle. The mountain Ill Bell (the Beltain Top) was probably used for fire worship.

The Northern and Southern Celts fought against each other at Barco Hill, near Penrith, for dominion of the race, and the South-erners from Cambria won. (It is from them that we have the name

Celtic settlement at Ewe Close, West Cumbria

'Cumbria'). When the Romans arrived from the south they erected a strong fort at Old Penrith between the Northern and Southern Celts, on the river Petteril (Celtic *Pedrogyl* – the quadrangle). The Celtic name of the fort was *Ceatheir Lean* (the square of the river), now Catterlen.

They had hillfort settlements at Carrock Fell, Caermote, near Bothel, Ewe Close, near Gilcrux, Moota Hill, near Blindcrake, and Blindcrake. All the names derived from Celtic ones. Blindcrake is derived from two Celtic words, *blaen* meaning summit, and *craic* or *craig*, meaning a crag. Isel on the Derwent are both Celtic words, Derwent meaning 'oak river'. The Triskele Stone, part of a Celtic cross, was for a good many years in Isel Church, but was stolen in 1986. (Three places in Austria also have the unusual name 'Isel', one near Innsbruck, another near Bregenz and the third near Lienz.)

The Brigantes made a vigorous and protracted resistance against the Roman invasion. Their metropolis was *Isurium Brigantium*, now Aldborough, near Boroughbridge, Yorkshire, and Cumberland was part of their territory. They were the last of the tribes to

Celtic artefacts in Tullie House Museum, Carlisle

51

Celtic artefacts in Tullie House Museum, Carlisle

The Isel Triskele Stone.
Thought to be part of an ancient
Celtic cross

capitulate to the Romans, under Petilius Cerealis, a celebrated commander, in AD 70.

After the Romans had left Britain, Brigantia became the kingdom of Rheged and it was king Urien of Rheged, a powerful warrior king, who drove the Saxons eastwards to the sea.

The Celts easily accepted Christianity. In the Hadrian's Wall region it was well established by the end of the 4th century.

Spanish and French Celts made their way up the river Derwent, and settled in Borrowdale.

King Urien's grandson, Duvenald (Dunmail), as king of Strathclyde, continued resisting the English. Edmund invaded Cumberland, giving it to Malcolm, king of the Scots. At the battle at 'Dunmail Raise', the British were defeated. Dunmail was not killed there, as is popularly thought, but Edmund blinded his two sons. Dunmail continued to rule Strathclyde for many years afterwards, and died in Rome whilst on a pilgrimage there.

The cairn on Dunmail Raise, now much reduced, marked the boundary between Cumberland and Westmorland.

Rhun, a son of king Urien of Rheged, is said to have baptised Edwin, king of the Saxons of Northumbria and 12,000 of his subjects.

About 635 Oswy, king of Northumbria, married Rieinmelch, granddaughter of Rhun, thus Rheged came under Anglican rule and became part of their kingdom about 930.

In the 10th century Strathclyde Britons re-conquered north Cumberland, where the Britons were a majority.

Bede, in his *Historia Ecclesiastica* in 731 wrote, 'Aethelfrith (593–616) conquered more territories from the Britons than any other chieftain or king, either subduing the inhabitants and making them tributory, or driving them out and planting the English in their place.'

The Cumbric language was spoken until the 11th century. (Latin was used by the upper classes until the 7th century, when Celtic once more became the courtly language.)

Celtic forts in NW Cumberland were at Snittlegarth, Whitehall, Weary Hall, Dovenby, Castlemont, Wolsty, Mawbray, Westnewton, Hayton and Brytaon, and at Castle Howe, Peel Wyke and Bassenthwaite.

Moota Hill beacon was the master beacon for Allerdale. There were several other beacons on the hill. Besides being the site of a Brigantian stronghold, Moota Hill was an ancient meeting place.

A fort was at Skelmore Heads, near Urswick, Furness, at the summit of Carrock Fell at 2,174 feet with a 5 acre walled settlement, at Castlehead, near Grange-over-Sands; Castlesteads, Nantland; Castle Crag, Mardale, at 1,250 feet; Castle Crag, Borrowdale and Shoulthwaite Gill, Thirlmere. Others were at Brough-under-Stainmore, Kirkby Thore and Stanwix and at Aughertree, near Uldale.

There were settlements in most Lakeland valleys. Stone walled ones with fields, containing one or more circular huts were to be found near Crosby Ravensworth, Ewe Close, Crosby Garrett and Asby. There was a palisaded enclosure at Wolsty Hall, Silloth, and a walled enclosure at Urswick Stone Walls, Furness. A settlement was at Stone Close, Stainton, and at the Hawk, Broughton Mills was an enclosure with circular stone based huts. At Holme Bank, Scales, was a small farm. On the Torver Back, Coniston, was an enclosure, and there were settlements at Satterthwaite, Nibthwaite, Stonestar and Caw, in Seathwaite and Dunnerdale, and at Crosbythwaite, Duddon. At Hugill near Windermere was a strong walled enclosure with circular stone huts inside, and at Millrigg, Kentmere, seven circular hut sites were found. There were also settlements at Longsleddale and Bannisdale, at Towtop Kirk near Shap, at Bampton, Skirsgill Hill, Askham and Yanwath, and at Brougham, Old Carlisle, Risehow, Maryport, and Rosley. At Threlkeld there was a settlement with circular stone huts within a wall, also at Stonecarr, Motherby, Hartsop, Brotherswater, Deepdale, Glencoyndale and Bannerdale. There were enclosures at Infell, Ponsonby, Hurlbarrow Farm, Bolton Wood, Gosforth, Barnscar and Brantrake Moss. Farms were at Waberthwaite and Devoke Water.

A pair of bronze bracelets were found near Thirlmere and a bronze bridle bit was found on Place Fell, Ullswater.

It is thought there would be a population of about 16,000 in the Lake District in the pre-Roman times, and in AD 1500 about 70/80,000.

During the Roman occupation the Celts would have to supply them with grain and lard, timber for fuel and building, minerals, horses and leather and recruits for the auxiliary forces.

Romanisation of the Celts would only take place along

Hadrian's Wall, at forts and at Carlisle, otherwise they did not alter their customary way of life and when the Romans left, and in AD 410 when Honorius informed the people of Britain they would in future have to defend themselves, this did not cause any hardship to the northern Celts who were well prepared to deal with enemy invasions.

Celtic river names are Eden, Lune, Kent, Crake, Esk, Calder, Ellen and Derwent. Celtic hill names are Blencathra, Carrock, Mell and Helvellyn, and Celtic village names are Glencoyne, Penruddock, Blennerhasset and Torpenhow.

Glyn was a valley, pen a head, blaen a top, tor a peak and caer a fort.

There were Pele Towers in Allerby, Oughterside, Bromfield, Crookdake and Brayton.

The Hibero-Celts founded Carlisle, Blencairn, Blindcrake, Cargo, Cardurnock, Lamplugh, Dundraw, Gilcrux and Gilgarren, and gave their names to Glencoin, Glenridding and Glendera-makin. The Cambrian Celts founded Old Penrith, and Penrud-dock, and gave their names to Cumrew and Helvellyn.

The Celtic church was most active in the Solway and Carlisle areas, as well as in the Eden Valley.

Leprosy came to Cumberland in the 10th century, and a Leper Hospital was built just outside Carlisle. It was founded by king Athelstan in 940, and dedicated to St Leonard. Lepers were also cared for at Holm Cultram Abbey. (King Robert Bruce of Scotland died of leprosy in 1327.) The Black Death reached Cumberland about 1350.

Up to about 100 years ago Cumberland sheep farmers still used the Celtic numerals to count their sheep.

1.	Yan	11.	Yan-a-dick
2.	Tyan	12.	Tyan-a-dick
3.	Tethera	13.	Tethera-a-dick
4.	Methera	14.	Methera-a-dick
5.	Pimp	15.	Bumfit
6.	Sethera	16.	Yan-a-bumfit
7.	Lethera	17.	Tyan-a-bumfit
8.	Hovera	18.	Tethera-a-bumfit
9.	Dovera	19.	Methera-a-bumfit
10.	Dick	20.	Giggot

8

The Roman Invasion of Britain

Having conquered Gaul Caesar turned his attention to Britain and in the autumn of 55 BC he crossed the Channel with eighty ships containing about 10,000 men, and 18 transports for the cavalry, and beached on the shore at Walmer, Kent, where the Britons were massed to meet them.

At first there was confusion amongst the Romans as they were attacked, but once they were all able to land and form up into their units, they charged the tribesmen who retired in disorder. After driving off the Britons the Romans made camp. A few days later a storm arose and damaged the Roman fleet. Whilst the 7th Legion was engaged in reaping corn, it was attacked by the Britons, but Roman reinforcements arrived and routed them. However, the Britons continued to attack the Roman camp, and as winter was approaching Caesar decided to withdraw, and he and his army returned to Gaul, having failed in his venture.

By the following year 600 ships and 28 transports had been constructed and on the 6th July 54 BC he set out for Britain once more with five legions (about 30,000 men) and 2,000 cavalry. They landed between Sandown Castle and Sandwich. A large force of Britons had gathered, but at the sight of the huge fleet, had retired into the woods. After midnight, leaving ten battalions and 300 cavalry to guard the fleet, the Romans moved off and after 12 miles, near Canterbury, met the Britons who attacked them from a strongly fortified position, but they were repulsed by the Roman cavalry and withdrew.

The main opposition to Caesar was the Catuvellanni tribe, under king Cassivelaunus, whose kingdom covered a large area of Hertfordshire and Essex, and whose capital was at Wheathampstead.

The 7th Legion attacked the British stronghold and took it and drove off the defenders. Next day the Roman cavalry set off to find them, but returned when news was received that their fleet

56

had been severely damaged by a storm, destroying 40 ships. The remainder were beached and surrounded by fortifications.

A large British force under Cassivelaunus attacked the main Roman army and engaged in guerrilla warfare, using war chariots and cavalry. The Romans continued their advance and crossed the Thames, in spite of its defences and a large British force there, and they eventually reached the British stronghold. This they attacked but the defenders escaped. This ended Caesar's advance, and he retraced his steps to the coast, where he found that the British had attacked his camp, but without success.

Cassivelaunus sent delegates to discuss terms of surrender. Caesar demanded hostages and an annual tribute and non-interference with the Trinovantes, who had sought Caesar's protection. It was now September and Caesar hurriedly departed with his damaged fleet and arrived safely in Gaul.

It was 97 years before the next Roman invasion took place. The Britons only paid the tribute for a short time, and resumed their normal activities once more.

At the time of Caesar's invasions the population consisted of Iron Age Britons and a small number of Belgae in Hertfordshire and along the Kent coast. When the Romans returned in 43 AD the Belgae had become an empire with an aristocracy, stretching over the whole of the south-west of England to the Bristol Channel, and north to the Wash.

50 years after Caesar's invasions, the Catuvellauni of Hertfordshire absorbed the Trinovantes of Essex and about AD 10 their king, Cunobelinus, established himself at Camulodunum (Colchester), named after their war god. He ruled an area covering the Chilterns, the lower Thames Valley, Essex and part of Kent. They struck their own coins.

In a rich grave at Lexden, Colchester, were found an iron bound litter, statuettes, silver studded chainmail and a bronze table.

A king of the Atrebates in an area in southern Surrey and Sussex, named Verica, was driven out by Cunobelinus in AD 41, and Verica fled to Rome and requested help. In that year Cunobelinus died, and there was a struggle for his successor.

The Dumnonii ruled in Devon and Cornwall, and the Dobunni in Somerset and Gloucestershire, the Iceni were in East Anglia, the Coritani in Leicestershire and Lincolnshire, and the Parisi in Yorkshire, whilst the Briganti ruled the large area of Lancashire, part Yorkshire, Westmorland, Co. Durham and Cumberland. The Silures were in Wales, also the Deceangli and Ordovices.

The Roman Occupation

In 43 AD Emperor Claudius despatched four legions to Britain intent on conquest.

They found no opposing army when they landed, it is thought, at Richborough, Dover and Lympne.

Caratacus and Togodumnus, sons of Cunobelinus, were both defeated, then part of Bodunni capitulated. After a two-day battle Caratacus withdrew to the Thames.

The Roman army camped near the Thames to wait the arrival of Claudius from Rome. Once there he led the army against the

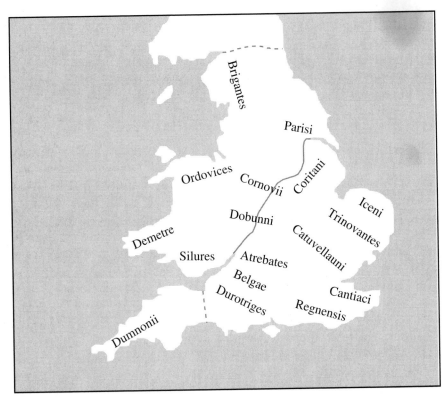

ROMAN BRITAIN

British stronghold of Camulodunum, which he captured and defeated its defenders. Many tribes capitulated or were overcome by force. Claudius only stayed in Britain for 16 days and then returned to Rome, leaving Plautius to complete the conquest of the country.

The Legions pushed northwards and to the north-west towards Lincoln and Wales, and westward towards Devon. Only the Durotriges of Dorset put up a strong resistance and the SE was easily conquered. It is chronicled that Vespian fought 30 battles, subjugated two tribes, the Durotriges and Belgae in Dorset and Wiltshire, and captured more than 20 strongholds and the Isle of Wight. King Cogeduminus, in Sussex, accepted Roman protection and Claudius made him his representative. King Prasutagus of the Iceni in East Anglia capitulated. The Dumnoni in Devon do not appear to have resisted.

When in AD 47 Aulus Plautius returned to Rome and was replaced by Publius Ostorius Scapula, several tribes, including the Iceni, the Deceangli and Ordivices and Demetae, and the Silures of Wales, revolted, but were suppressed by the new commander who reduced the territory as far as the Trent and Severn. Two battalions were ambushed and annihilated in south Wales. Some of the Brigantes rebelled but without success. The Romans drew up a frontier called the Fosse Way, stretching from Lincoln to Exeter. Because this frontier was constantly harassed by the Welsh, the Romans invaded south Wales, and then in the north, and finally, in AD 61 overcame the Druid stronghold of Anglesey, after much slaughter and they chopped down the oak groves, which were sacred to the Druids.

Caratacus, who had been carrying on guerrilla warfare, was commander of a hillfort in Wales when it was attacked by the Romans, who, after a desperate fight, overcame it. However, Caratacus escaped captive and fled to the Brigantes. Their Queen, Cartimandua, however, handed him over to the Romans, and he was taken in chains to Rome by Ostorius. (The war had lasted nine years so far.) Caratacus and his family were paraded through the streets of Rome, and brought before Claudius. He, however, pardoned them all and they were allowed to live in Italy.

Because of trouble in Brigantia in AD 57 between Queen Cartimandua and her divorced consort, Venutius, the Romans intervened, marching from Lincoln, and defending her from the attacks by Venutius. She had married his armour bearer, and was pro-Roman, whilst Venutius was anti-Roman, and was in control of most of Brigantia.

The Romans built a network of roads throughout their conquered territories and encouraged the Britons to leave their hillforts and settlements and build new towns on the Roman plan. St Albans, Silchester, Chichester and Cirencester were the first British towns to be built.

In AD 60 king Prasutagus of the Iceni, in East Anglia, had died leaving half his kingdom to the Romans and half to his two daughters. However, the Romans claimed all, and when his widow, Queen Boudicca, protested, she was flogged and her daughters raped.

Boudicca rallied an army and vent on revenge, set forth. Her force, which had swollen to 120,000 tribesmen, first attacked Camulodunum, occupied by Roman and British and as it was a new town there were no defence works. After a two day siege, the Britons broke into the town and put it to flames. The survivors took refuge in the huge Roman Temple but this too was destroyed, and all those in it massacred. After looting the town the force moved on. St Albans fell to them, and met the same fate as Camulodunum.

A Roman force of 2,000 men and some cavalry left their camp at Lincoln, and hurried south to intercept Boudicca's force, but were surrounded and annihilated, except for the cavalry which escaped.

Another Roman force hurried from north Wales to London, ahead of Boudicca's force, but the commander decided not to defend the town, but departed together with most of the inhabitants. Those who remained in London were slaughtered and the town put to flames. In all 70,000 were lost.

The Roman army of only 10,000 men under Suetonius Paullinus, had chosen an advantageous site near Lichfield, which could only be attacked from the front, to give battle to the Britons, and they stood their ground as the Britons hurled themselves upon them. The battle continued all day long, and in the end the Britons fled in disorder, having lost 80,000 men. Boudicca took poison to avoid capture.

Boudicca (the name means 'Victory'), the warrior Queen of the Iceni tribe, and a high priestess was described by Tacitus thus,

'She was huge of frame, terrifying of aspect, and with a harsh voice. A great mass of bright red hair fell to her knees, and she wore a great twisted golden necklace, and a tunic of many colours, over which was a thick mantle, fastened by a brooch.'

Ammianus Marcellinus, the 4th century Greek historian, stated this about Celtic women. 'Almost all are of tall stature, fair and ruddy, terrible for the fierceness of their eyes, fond of quarrelling, and of overbearing insolence. In a fight she swells her neck and gnashes her teeth and poising her huge white arms, begins to rain blows mingled with kicks like shots discharged by a catapult.'

Fresh reinforcements were sent from the continent to bring the Roman forces up to their full complement again, and a new Governor was sent from Rome to pursue a policy of moderation.

London, St Albans and Colchester were rebuilt, and new towns and villas appeared. *Pax Romana* came into being.

As the Brigantians had a large army, and as the Romans regarded them as unreliable, they decided that they would have to suppress them. Their capital was Isurium Brigantium, now Aldborough, Yorkshire. In AD 71 a Roman force set out from Borough on Humber for Newcastle-on-Tyne, via York, where they built a fortress and from there they attacked the Brigantians under Venutius and several battles took place. It is thought that Venutius's stronghold was at Sandwick, a huge fortified camp, where he could make his last stand. The Romans stormed it in AD 72, and overcame it, and Venutius perished with his garrison, and the Romans moved further north to the Tyne.

In AD 79 Agricola's force moved up the western side from north Wales, which he had conquered, to Carlisle, and all Brigantia was subdued but not pacified. A line of forts was built from Carlisle to Newcastle.

Roman forces pushed further north following the western and eastern routes. The lowland tribes, the Novantae, Segolvae, Votandiui and Dumnoni all submitted to them. The Novantae were in south Ayrshire, Dumfriesshire and Galloway. The Votandiui were in the Lothians, the Dumnoni in Renfrewshire and Dumbartonshire. They were probably treaty States to the Romans. In AD 81 the Romans reached the Clyde and Forth, where they built a line of forts, which later on (AD 141) became the Antonine Line, which extended from Bridgeness on the Forth to Old Kilpatrick on the Clyde.

In 83/84 Agricola advanced still further north into Scotland, and reached Inchtuthill, having already been attacked by the Caledonians under Calgacus. A legion was left there in winter quarters. In the lower reaches of the Clyde there were a number of hillforts, the most important being Walls Hill, Renfrewshire, held by the Dumnoni.

In 84 Calgacus gathered a force of 30,000 men and chariots at the Graupian Mountain. Agricola brought 20,000 men and 3,000 cavalry to do battle against them. The Romans attacked. At first the Britons held their position, but Roman cavalry disorganised them into groups which the Romans overcame. The rest of the Britons retreated to the woods and hills, leaving 10,000 dead. This was the last battle of the invasion, and the Romans did not advance beyond this point. The threat of the Caledonians was broken, for the time being anyway, but this was to remain a frontier zone with hostile tribes to the north of it. It had taken 41 years to subdue Britain, Wales and most of Scotland, although there were always to remain pockets of resistance.

In the early occupation of Scotland pile dwellings were common on the Lochs, and caves were often used.

The remains of a 4th century silver table service were found on Traprain Law in 1919.

9

After the Roman Conquest

The Roman conquest brought little change to the Celtic tribes and their way of life, except in SE Britain, where they gradually became Romanised and began to use Latin.

Hadrian's Wall, 73½ miles long, was completed about AD 130 and required 12,000 men to garrison it.

The Antonine Line was built 141. The latter was in time abandoned and the Romans retreated to Hadrian's Wall, which became their northern frontier. It was constantly under attack from the Scots and Picts from the north, and from time to time they broke through.

There were Celtic uprisings in 155 and 181. In 208 the Romans subdued the Caledonii in Perthshire and the Picts in the Lowlands. However, the British tribes between the two walls were left to look after themselves.

In the 3rd and 4th centuries of the Roman occupation relative peace reigned in northern Roman Britain.

Meanwhile the Romans were under great pressure on the Continent, their northern frontier being under attack, and Gaul in rebellion.

The Irish began raiding SW Wales in about 275, and they settled in Pembroke and Caernarvonshire. The Britons and Romans joined forces against the new threat. New forts were built at Cardiff, Holyhead and Caenarvon, also at Lancaster, Piercebridge and Elslack.

At the same time there were Pictish raids in the north. Hadrian's Wall was restored, and forts at High Rochester and York were built. 'The forts of the Saxon shore', from Norfolk to Hampshire were also a protection from attack by sea. However, all these measures in the end failed to keep out the raiders. In 367 the Irish, Picts and Saxons struck and penetrated deeply inland. Many towns were destroyed, but Carlisle, York, Chester and Leicester survived. Again Hadrian's Wall was repaired, but defensive posts north of it were abandoned. Signal stations on the Yorkshire coast were destroyed by the Saxons in 390.

In 383 Magnus Maximus was acclaimed Emperor and left for Gaul with his troops, although some were left behind. He was killed in 388 at Aquileia. Stilicho arrived in Britain in 395 and took charge of the defences, basing his northern command at York. (In 409/10 Rome was sacked by Alaric, the Goth, and Britain was also heavily raided.)

In 407, Constantine, a Roman soldier in Britain, was acclaimed Emperor and departed for Gaul with troops for the defence of the Rhine. However, he was defeated and slain. Thus ended Roman domination in Britain. In 410 came the rescript of Honorius, which informed the cities of Britain that they must look after themselves. The civil administration continued to about 418, when the Council of the Seven Provinces was held at Arles.

10

After the Romans

By the middle of the 4th century German tribes once more invaded Gaul. Visigoths, Ostrogoths and Vandals harassed the Roman Empire. In 406 Vandals, Alans and Lugi crossed the Rhine and made their way through Gaul and Spain. Visigoths settled in Narbonenses, whilst Burgundians went into Alsace. By the middle of the 5th century Roman Gaul ceased to exist.

In Britain, in 367 there were attacks from Saxons, Franks, Jutes and Angles who poured into the South and East and settled there. On the western seaboard there were incursions by the Irish.

As protection against Pictish raids the Britons invited Saxons to settle and repel the raiders. However, the Saxons soon complained that their supplies were inadequate, and for a time they devastated the countryside. The British were victorious at the battle of Mount Badon in 500, but cities were deserted and devastated. A widespread plague in 549 caused a large loss of life. The English settlers advanced westward and reached the boundaries of Wales and Cornwall. Meanwhile Irish settlers in large numbers arrived in Scotland, Wales and Cornwall.

From the middle of the 5th century to the founding of the Saxon kingdoms, all Britain was governed by the native Celtic princes once more and the Celtic language and culture became again supreme.

The heathen Celtic religion had survived the Roman occupation. The temple of Lydney on the Severn, built about 365 was constructed within an Iron Age hillfort.

Central and SE Britain were the most Romanised, and were able to continue an organised civil life, but Northern and Western Britain, and most of Wales were less Romanised, and had no secure self governing system.

However, in the matter of defence, the Celts were well prepared against their old enemies, the Picts, the Irish and the Saxons.

In the north the Strathclyde Celts, with their stronghold at

Dumbarton, held back the Picts. Bede refers to this kingdom *Dun Breataun*, as being very strongly fortified. In Wales the Princes were strong enough to keep out invaders from the sea, but Vortigern, a very powerful Prince, employed Saxon mercenaries to strengthen his armies.

According to Gildas, at the end of the 5th century, Devon and Cornwall was ruled by Constantine, SE Wales by Aurelius Caninus, Pembrokeshire by Vorteporius, West Wales by Cuneglasus, North Wales and Anglesey by Maglocunis. In the north west was the large kingdom of Rheged, ruled by king Urien. In 516, at the battle of Mount Badon, the Saxons were slaughtered.

It has been suggested that 'King Arthur' was in fact King Urien, who was based at Carlisle.

The Celts had sea-going vessels, and there was constant traffic between NE Ireland and SW Scotland. Continuous Irish settlement took place in Cornwall and in South and West Wales. In the 5th and 6th centuries migrations took place from SW Britain to Armorica in Gaul, the future Brittany, due no doubt to pressure from the Irish.

Scotland was traditionally the land of the Picts, so called by the Romans as they painted themselves, but they called themselves *Cruithni*. They had their own language, which has been lost and only a few carved stones remain with undecipherable inscriptions. By the 5th century they only occupied the northern part of Scotland, apart from the kingdom of Argyll north of the Antonine Wall. In the 6th century St Columba visited king Brude mac Maelchon, the Pict.

King Ecgfrith of Northumbria gradually extended his kingdom northwards and made serious inroads into the British kingdom, until in 685 he was slain at Forfar when warring against the Picts.

Part of Argyll, the kingdom of Cinel Gabrain, was Irish speaking and Columba ordained Aedan as king who remained loyal to him. (The Venerable Bede, who died 735, knew Britain as *Alba*, and the Irish named it as *Alba* until the 10th century.)

The eastern British were known as the Gododdin (Votadiui), whilst those in the west, the Strathclyde Britons, the Cymry, stretched from the Clyde to Mercia. Their old name was Cumbroges (Cumbrians). The Welsh called them *Gwyr y Gogledd* (the men of the north).

These Britons were both literate and Christian, but apart from a few stone inscriptions no written records exist, until the 7th century when Nennius includes some in his *Historia Brittonium*. The most important of the Cumbrian Princes was Urien of Rheged, centred at Carlisle, and his territory probably extended from Galloway to the Ribble, and from the Solway coast to Catterick, Yorkshire. According to Nennius he was the greatest of all warrior Princes and that he fought with three other British Princes, Rhydderch, Gwallane and Morcant, against Hussa, king of Bernicia (north Northumbria), and besieged him for three days and nights on the island of Metcand (Lindisfarne), but he, Urien, was murdered by Morcant. Urien's head was taken away by his cousin. The 'Lament of Urien of Rheged' goes 'A head I carry close to my side, Head of Urien, generous leader of hosts.'

After losing their leader the Britons were no longer effective against the Anglo-Saxons. At the battle of Arvarterid (Arthuret), near Longtown, Prince Gwenddolen was slain and it is said that Myrdden (Merlin) on losing his master, lost his wits and thenceforth lived as a wild man in the Forest of Celyddon (Caledonia).

There was a disastrous British expedition made by the men of Manau Gododdin into Northumbria and in their battle against the Angles they were annihilated.

Slowly the Angles regained their lost ground, and extended their territory up the south eastern side of Scotland, and by the beginning of the 7th century king Aethelfrith was ruler of the whole area. This advance into British territory resulted in migrations to Ireland and the Isle of Man. However, the western British kingdoms kept their independence until Riemmelth married king Osury of Northumbria, and thus Rheged became part of Northumbria, and the British and Angles had a peaceful union.

Strathclyde kept its independence for centuries, and the Angles northward thrust ended when Osury's son Ecgfrith was slain, but they still retained the Scottish Lowlands.

11

Wales

The northern Britons and those in Wales always kept in close communication with each other and probably the sea route was the easiest way to travel.

Nennius in his *Historia Brittonium* tells of Cunedag and eight sons and a grandson coming from Manau Guotodin to settle in Wales in the 5th century.

After the departure of the Romans Wales was divided amongst many little kingdoms, each with its own ruler. Demetia (Dyfed) had a dynasty which lasted from the fifth to the tenth century. The kingdom of Brycheiniog (Brecknock) also lasted until the 10th century. The church of Mynyar later became the Cathedral of St David.

Wales derives its name from the Anglo-Saxon *Wealh*, meaning foreigners. The Welsh called it *Cymru*, and themselves *Cymry*.

There was a gradual unification of Wales during the 9th and 10th centuries, until the final union with England under Athelstan, mainly due to inter-marriages, as they remained intact over many centuries. The union with England took place under Hywd Dda. A generation before, Alfred the Great did much to influence the movement towards union.

King Cadfan's son, the great Cadwallon, the greatest enemy of the English, was killed at the battle of Hexham in 633, when defeated by king Oswald of Northumbria.

Cyngen, the last king of Powys, died in 855 on a pilgrimage to Rome. His sister married Merfyn, whose court became a meeting place for Irish scholars on their way to the Continent. Merfyn died in 844. His son, Rhodri Mawr, ruled until 878, but during his reign he was constantly harried by Mercia and the Danes. Rhodri became the greatest power in Wales and his greatest antagonist was Alfred the Great. Anglesey had been devastated in 854 and Rhodri was forced to take refuge in Ireland for a time. Both he and his son Gwriad were killed by the Saxons.

After the death of Rhodri his kingdom was divided between his sons, who harassed the South Welsh kings, who favoured union with the English. They in turn appealed to Alfred for protection. Alfred too was kept occupied with his old eastern enemy, the Danes. He made an annual contribution to the Irish Church, but was in a close relationship with the Welsh. He invited Asser, the Welsh scholar of St David's, to spend part of his time at his court.

Hywel Dda, grandson of Rhodri, was leader in the first part of the 10th century. He had added SW Wales to his kingdom, and married the daughter of Dyfed. From 942 he was virtually the ruler of Wales under the English king Athestan. He died 950.

Gruffud ap Llywelyn, last High King of Wales was killed in 1063. The last Celtic Prince of Wales Llywelyn II died in 1282.

In pre-Norman Wales the people were divided into three classes, the free tribesmen who were dominant, the unfree, who carried on the agricultural work, and the slaves, who did most of the manual labour and were the property of their owners.

The fines system in their legal laws were laid down for exact payment for injury to the limbs and body of the victims.

Much of early Welsh poetry is preserved in four manuscripts dating from 1150 to 1350. Nennius gives the names of four famous bards, Talhiern Tataguen, Neirin, Taliesin and Blackbard. Nennius was a 9th century Welsh Celtic monk who collected various historical documents into his *Historia Brittonium*.

In 1176 the Lord Rhys held the first Eisteddfod at Cardigan. In 1200 Llywelyn the Great became Master of Gwynedd. He died in 1240.

The Welsh code of laws was the most important survival of Celtic Britain. It is claimed to have been instituted by Hywel Dda, the South Welsh king. Although there were written versions none survived, and it was after 1150 that we find manuscripts of later compilations. Hywel Dda's court of law consisted of 24 officials and their duties were laid down. There was a 'chief of song' and a bard appointed to the royal family, both privileged positions. There was a penal code setting out the penalties. Another section dealt with valuations and fines.

In 1471 Edward IV created the first Council of Wales. The first Act of Union with England was in 1536, the second was in 1543. In 1546 the first book was printed in Welsh. In 1588 Bishop

Morgan produced his Welsh Bible. The Act for Propagation of the Gospel in Wales was in 1650. In 1688 was the Toleration Act. The beginning of the Methodist revival was in 1735.

12

The Early Church

It is not exactly known when Christianity was introduced into Britain, but it is thought that it was already established by the 2nd century. Three British bishops were summoned to the Council of Arles in 314, and Rimini in 359. In the 5th century the northern half of Ireland was converted by St Patrick, a native it is thought of the Solway region of Strathclyde. The southern part of Ireland was probably already Christian. Wales was probably Christian from Roman times. The earliest missionary in northern Britain was St Ninian, who built a church of stone at Whithorn.

The earliest Welsh saint was Dubricuss, with churches on the River Wye. His pupil, St Illtud, became the first Abbot of Llantwit Major monastery, and one of his pupils was St Samson. The early Cornish church seems to have arisen out of Welsh connections. The sculptured crosses of both countries are very similar in style. It would seem that the conversion of the Isle of Man would come from Whithorn on the Solway, although their early Celtic chapels the *keeills*, are very similar to those in the Orkneys. The remains of over 170 have been identified.

The 6th century in the Celtic church is known as the 'Age of the Saints', as a religious enthusiasm led to a rise of monasteries. This first began in the late Roman period in Egypt, and from there spread into Palestine, Syria, Mesopotamia, Italy, Gaul, Spain and Brittany. Many cells and sanctuaries were founded along these coastlines. Well known was that founded by St Honotartus, off Cannes, in about 410.

In Britain, many islands around its coasts were occupied, the best known being Iona. Another was Skellig Michael, off the coast of Co. Kerry, where the cells, chapel and graveyard can still be seen. It was built in the 6th or 7th century. It is a bare rock 700 ft high in the Atlantic, eight miles from the Irish coast. It is the most perfectly preserved of all the island sites. Six beehive cells and two small oratories are still intact. There is also a tiny burial plot and some stone slabs with crosses. There are 600 steps up to the monastery site.

Bardsey Island, off the Caernarvon coast, is said to have 20,000 saints buried there. Caldy Island and Lindisfarne are also well-known places which were occupied. Glastonbury and Tintagel also had large communities.

Well known Saints were St Martin of Tours, St Finian of Clonard, St Dyfrig of Trenllan, St Samson of Dol, St Columba of Iona, St Kentigern of Hoddom then Glasgow, St Serf of Culross, St Fructuosus of Spain, St Boniface, St Fridolin, St Columbanus of Bobbio, Kilian of Würzburg, Fursa of Péroune, Fiacra, Gall and Donatus of Fiesole. In Cumberland were St Bridget, St Bega, St Sancton, St Cuthbert and St Herbert.

St Columba had the reputation of being the greatest saint in the Celtic Church, and it was in Iona that the greatest developments took place. His birthplace is thought to have been at Gartan in Donegal, and he was a Prince of the northern Ui Neill. In 563 he sailed to the kingdom of Dalriada in Scotland, with twelve disciples, and founded the monastery on Iona, and then proceeded to convert the Northern Picts. Iona became the head of the Celtic Church in Ireland, Scotland and England. Iona gave sanctuary to the exiled king Oswald of Northumbria, and when he returned to his kingdom in 634, he invited Aidan and 12 monks to settle at Lindisfarne. St Columba exerted great influence in Western Scotland, and the church spread rapidly there. He died in 597.

Kilmacolm, near the Clyde, means 'the cell of Columba'. St Columba, so it is said, saw the Loch Ness monster, which had killed one of his followers and whom he restored to life again. St Columba made the sign of the cross over the monster and it then kept away.

The same year, 597, Augustine arrived in Kent from Rome. He was received by king Ethelbert, who gave him permission to settle in Canterbury. The king was soon converted. In 601 Augustine was appointed Archbishop. The king of the East Saxons was converted, and within 40 years most of the English had been introduced to Roman Christianity. Thus, Augustine founded the church which spread throughout Britain, and which superseded the Celtic Church, but not without some difficulties, as many in the Celtic Church had no desire to change to the different order of the Roman Church.

With the help of Aidan of Iona, Northumbria was finally converted to Christianity by king Oswald (634 to 641). Oswald had lived in exile in Scotland, and had been converted by the monks of Iona. It was the Celtic form of Christianity that came there.

From Lindisfarne, in Northumbria, many missionaries went out to convert other areas of England, and Christianity spread to south of the Humber, and this Celtic Christianity remained independent of Canterbury until 699.

One difficulty between the Celtic and Roman Churches was the dating of Easter. In the early 7th century Rome and Canterbury were urging the Irish and British to conform with the Catholic Church over this matter. By 629 most of southern Ireland conformed with Rome, but it took another 60 years before the north did, mainly due to Ecgberht, a Northumbrian monk, and the Abbot of Iona, Adamnan. However, it was not until 716 that the church of Iona fully accepted the Roman order.

After the Synod of Whitby (663), the Roman form spread gradually throughout the country and Western Europe. The Celtic Church established in Spanish Galicia in the 6th century, accepted the Roman order at the 4th Council of Toledo in 633 and by the middle of the 8th century most of the churches in Europe had accepted it. However, in Britain the change took longer, and half a century was to pass after Whitby, before the southern Picts accepted. Wales accepted in 665.

This controversy stimulated the Celtic Church to set down in writing their traditions and culture, which until then had been largely transmitted orally. This resulted in a great intellectual exercise which left its mark in history. Thus ended the Celtic Church in Britain.

About 685 St Adamnan wrote a biography of St Columba, 'Dove of the Church'.

13

Cornwall

Emigrants, mainly Belgic tribes, from northern and western France and Belgium settled in strength in southern Britain. They came in three waves, the first in the 5th and 4th centuries BC, the second in the south-west in the 3rd and 2nd centuries BC, and lastly in the late 2nd to the mid 1st century BC, due to invasions by Germanic tribes, the Cimbri and Teutons, into Gaul, in 120 to 110 BC, and the invasions of Julius Caesar in 58 to 50 BC. These emigrants were known as the Dumnonii, as named by Ptolemy. They carried on a flourishing trade in tin for the Mediterranean market through Gallic merchants. Agriculture however was the main occupation, with stock keeping predominant. They lived in open settlements in round huts and cultivated small fields. They had brought with them a knowledge of iron. In the metalworker's hut at Kestor, there was a small bowl furnace full of iron slag, a forging pit, a quenching place and an anvil stone. Iron ore was obtained from the Hennock area.

They re-introduced inhumation burial. A large cemetery was found in 1900 to 1905 at Harlyn Bay. Here the bodies were buried in a contracted position in coffins of slate slabs, with grave goods (bronze and iron pins, brooches, earrings and a bracelet), from the late 4th and 3rd centuries BC. Other cemeteries were at Mount Batten, Plymouth and Trelan Bahow, St Keverne, where there were rich female graves, with bracelets, beads, brooches, mirrors and glass vessels. There was a midden beside the Harlyn Bay cemetery. From the local slate needles, awls, loomweights and spindle whorls were made. There were also bone weaving combs and bobbins, and decorated pottery. Dyes were used to colour cloth.

There was a trading settlement at Mount Batten. At the close of the 3rd century BC, Blackbury Castle, a four-acre fortified site was built. At Maen Castle, Land's End, a promontory was fortified, using a wall of granite blocks and earth. Nearby were small terraced fields.

By the 2nd century BC trade routes were established between the Mediterranean and SW Britain, through Gallic merchants. A hoard of 43 silver drachmae was found at Paul, Penzance, minted by Celts in Cisalpine Gaul. Ingots of tin, for export, weighed 158 lbs. These were transported to St Michael's Mount. Decorated pottery was made in the Meare and Glastonbury areas.

Large hillforts are at Dumpdon, Hembury, Trevelegue, Carnyke, Countisbury, Sidbury, Musbury, Worlebury, Gurnard's Head, Treacrom, Drewerstone and Chun. There are numerous other smaller forts. The earliest wooden huts were 20 to 30 ft in diameter. A decorated bronze shield mount was found at Caerloggas hillfort, St Mawgan-in-Pyder. At Hengistbury Head fort silver and copper coins were minted. A hoard of 12 iron currency bars was found at Holne Chase hillfort. Two hoards of coins were found in 1749 in Carn Brea hillfort, Camborne. The Dumnonii never had a coinage.

In the 1st century BC schools of metal workers were established in southern Britain, producing articles for the aristocracy. North Somerset was a region of bronze workers, whilst the south-west region specialized in mirrors. A decorated sword scabbard was found in peat on Meare Heath in 1928, and has been dated to the late 2nd or early 1st century BC. The same style was found on a mirror in a woman's grave at Trelan Bahow, the Lizard. A ceremonial bronze collar was found in a stream at Trenoweth, Lelant. A bronze bowl was found in a bog at Youlton, probably a votive offering.

After the invading Roman armies had conquered the Durotriges and the western Belgic tribes, the Second Augustan Legion under Vespasian attacked the south-west and overcame 20 hillforts, including Maiden Castle, and conquered the Isle of Wight, and the Dumnonii soon submitted. By AD 47–48 the conquest of the west country was almost completed. The Romans decided to turn the conquered southern area into an Imperial Province and founded a new town at Exeter, as administrative headquarters for the Dumnonii. It took its name from the River Exe – *Isca Dumnoniorum*. Rectangular timber houses and workshops were built on each side of a narrow road leading to the river crossing. They had a frame of wooden posts with wattle and daub walls with Roman roof tiles. They were occupied from AD 50 to 75, and were destroyed by fire about AD 80. Between 80 and 85 the site was cleared and stone buildings erected. The town had no defences until the middle of the second century, when a rampart and ditch were built around it and about 200 a stone wall was added. The Council was responsible for the assessment and collection of taxes throughout the Canton, which included all the Cornish peninsular. In Cornwall five Roman milestones from the 3rd and 4th centuries indicate that it was included in the new Roman road system.

There was little change in the lifestyle of the Dumnonii, and they continued to live in their round stone huts in small groups, and to till their small fields. Good examples are at Porth and Crane Godrevy, west Cornwall, which were occupied from the 2nd to the 4th centuries AD. Mainly local pottery still continued to be used. Some of the western hillforts, such as Carn Brea and Trevelgue, continued to be inhabited throughout the 1st and 2nd centuries.

The Romans prospected for metals in mid-Cornwall between 60 and 70 AD, but they were not interested in tin, as they had ample supplies from northern Spain. However, when that source became exhausted in the mid-third century, Cornish tin was again in demand, and the tin streams in mid-Cornwall were worked. A 4th century 40 lb tin ingot, with Imperial inscription, was found at Carnanton, St Mawgan-in-Pyder. A pewter cup was found at Halviggan, St Stephen-in-Brannel, and a coin hoard with a metal dish, dated 3rd century, at Carnon, Devoran. A hoard of 1,600 coins was found in a pot under a stone near Breagne. Another six coin hoards were found in Cornwall dating from the 4th century.

The Cornish tin of the late 3rd and 4th centuries was also used for pewter jugs and dishes, and were made at Lansdown, Bath, and Camerton, where stone moulds were found. A tin flagon, containing 2,500 coins of 250–75 AD, was found at Carhazes, south Cornwall, hidden under stones.

The land of the Dumnonii under Roman rule remained backward and poor.

After the breakdown of Roman rule, Celtic Christianity was strengthened by contacts with western and southern Gaul. Christianity began in Dumnonia in late Roman times, but it spread generally in the 6th century due to missionary monks from South Wales, Ireland and Brittany. Celtic churches took the name of their founder. In Cornwall 174 out of 212 ancient parishes are dedicated to a western saint.

St Samson of South Wales (480–560 AD), landed at Padstow and travelled overland and first met the pagan people at Trig Major. At the end of his mission he embarked for Dol in Brittany. Another Welsh missionary, St Paul Aurelian, followed in his footsteps, and went to Ushant and Saint Pol de Léon. Another, St Petroc, remained in Cornwall, and founded a monastery near Padstow, and later went to Bodmin in the mid 6th century. There were other missions to mid and east Cornwall. Irish missionaries who founded St Breaca of Bregue, and St Hya of St Ives, were in west Cornwall. Saints from Brittany were St Winwaloe at Gunwalloe, St Corentin at Cury, and St Rumon at Tavistock.

The mission settlements were very primitive, with a little church and cell huts for each monk. These were usually built of stone and clay, with beaten earth floors and thatched roofs.

Dumnonia was a country of petty kings, and independent local dynasties when the West Saxons arrived and could offer no effective resistance.

When the Roman Emperor Honorius wrote to Britain in AD 410, informing it that it must now fend for itself, Cornwall retained its independence until the 9th or 10th century, when king Egbert (AD 834 to 39), and then king Athelstan (924 to 39) overcame Celtic resistance.

For 300 years before the reign of the Saxon king Egbert, there was a continuous struggle between the Britons and Saxons and many Britons left Cornwall to settle in Armorica (Brittany). The Britons were defeated at the battle of Deorham in 577 AD and this caused the permanent separation of the southern Britons and the Welsh. King Athelstan defeated Howel, the last king of Cornwall, and Cornwall became dominated by the Saxons. The monastic centres were reformed on Saxon lines and the Cornish became serfs under Saxon masters. The *Domesday Book* shows that most of the landowners were Saxon or Norman.

In 1050 the Bishopric of Cornwall was transferred to Exeter, Devon. The suppression of the Cornish by the Saxons in east Cornwall led to the loss of the Cornish language as a common tongue there. In west Cornwall the language survived longer, but in 1362 a statute was passed which directed all pleas in Courts of Justice to be made in English, thus making the official language English, but the poorer classes still used Cornish, until the 17th century. John Ray, in 1667, records that few children could speak Cornish 'so that the language is like in a short time to be quite lost'. In 1700 Cornish was still spoken in 25 parishes, but in 1735 very few could be found in the same parishes, due it is thought to the failure of parents to speak Cornish to their children. The opening up of America led to emigration of many Cornish-speaking people.

After the Reformation the very long intercourse between Cornwall and Brittany ceased, thus isolating Cornwall.

In his *Booke of the Introduction of Knowledge*, Andrew Borda in 1542 wrote, 'In Cornwall is two speches, the one is naughty Englysshe, and the other is Cornysshe speche. And there be many men and women the which cannot speake one worde of Englysshe, but all Cornysshe.'

The Civil War (1642–1651) saw the loss of many Cornishmen at the battle of Lansdown.

The Rev. John Whitaker (1735–1808) wrote 'English was forced upon the Cornish by the tyranny of England at a time when the English language was yet unknown in Cornwall.'

When George Fox visited St Ives and Marazion in 1640 he

spoke in support of the Quaker use of the second person singular, when Cornish was referred to.

In 1860, a memorial to Dolly Pentreath, reputed to be the last native speaker of Cornish, was raised by Prince Lucien Bonaparte.

14

The Celtic Saints

St Patrick

He was born about 390 AD in the Solway region, it is thought, the son of a Roman official. When nearly 16 he was made captive by Irish raiders and taken back to Ireland, where he was put to work as a cattle herd. He was six years in slavery, and then in a dream he was urged to return home, and told 'the ship is ready'. He escaped and travelled 200 miles to the ship he dreamt about. He went aboard and was landed in France. He returned to Britain and rejoined his family, after walking for 28 days.

After receiving heavenly instructions to return to Ireland, he entered the priesthood and then returned to Ireland, where he converted many tribal kings and their people. The church he founded was based on the Roman British one. He died in 460.

St Ninian

He was trained at Rome, and it is said his father was a Christian king. He brought the faith to the southern Picts. When he returned from a visit to Rome he went to the monastery of Tours, where St Martin had died in 397. He brought back masons from there to build his church of St Martin at Whithorn, in Galloway, which was under the rule of king Tadovallus and Ninian converted him.

It is said he had a cell on the bank of a stream, Mellendonor, which flowed into the Clyde. Towards the end of the 4th century he moved to Galloway. After his departure the Clyde area became heathen once more and remained so until the arrival of Kentigern one and a half centuries later. St Ninian was the first missionary to Cumberland and he preached by the River Eamont in the 4th century. He is associated with Ninekirks, Brisco and Brampton, where the church is dedicated to St Martin. There was also a well known as Ninewells, and there was once an oak tree known as St Martin's Oak. He died in 432.

St Bega

Tradition has it that she was an Irish Princess, who fled to sea, to escape from a Norwegian suitor, and she vowed that if God saved her she would devote the rest of her life in prayer, wherever she was cast ashore. The small boat she was in came ashore at what is now known as St Bees Head. That she begged the Lord of Egremont to grant her some land on which she could build a hermitage, and that he said she could have all the land on which it snowed next day. As it was Midsummer Day he did not expect any snow, but it did snow, and covered three miles as far as Whitehaven. So Bega's wish was granted, and she was able to build her nunnery. She died in 630. Later, in the reign of Henry I, it became the site of St Bees Priory.

It is said that prayers to St Bega brought healing to the deaf, dumb, blind and demented. There was a statue of her, a finger of which oozed oil, it was said.

Tradition also has it that there was an arm ring of St Bega kept in the Priory and oaths were sworn upon it. These rings were usually embossed with a cross. 'The bracelet of the blessed Virgin Bega', as it was known.

In 1315 raiding Scots took away all the vestments, and it is thought St Bega's ring was also taken by them.

St Bees Church is dedicated to St Bega. There is also a St Begh's Church in Egremont, and a St Bega's Church at Bassenthwaite.

St Cuthbert

He was bishop of Lindisfarne from 685 to 687 and received the gift of Carlisle from king Ecgfrith with the land 15 miles around. He visited the town in 685 and restored a decaying nunnery, and instituted a school there and was shown the Roman fountain in the market place. He paid annual visits to St Herbert, who had a cell on an island in Derwentwater. St Herbert made a wish that they should both be taken by the Lord on the same day, and according to the Venerable Bede this came to pass, on the 19th March 687.

In 875 the monks left Lindisfarne taking his body with them, to

Lindisfarne Priory. 12th century

Lindisfarne Priory. 9th century gravestone. Vikings attacking the monks

escape from the Vikings. They travelled to the mouth of the Derwent intending to cross over to Ireland, but were driven back by storms, and so made their way to Chester-le-Street.

He was born about 634 possibly of princely stock. One day whilst looking after sheep he had a heavenly vision, after which he went to Melrose and became a monk there. He devoted his life to prayer, and it is said performed many miracles. Eventually he became prior and made many missionary journeys.

After the Synod of Whitby, 664, he went to Lindisfarne, and later became a hermit on one of the Farne Islands, living in a very primitive cell in the rock. He was visited from time to time by the monks of Lindisfarne. Later he was appointed Bishop of Lindisfarne but was very reluctant to leave his hermitage. However, in 685 he agreed and was consecrated that Easter, 26th March in York. He now began a repetition of evangelistic journeys in the area, in which miracles and healings took place. After Christmas 686 he resigned and returned to his old hermitage where he remained until his death on 20th March 687.

The Lindisfarne monks prepared his body and dressed it in his

Statue of St Cuthbert – Durham Cathedral

priestly garments, and laid it in a stone sarcophagus there, on the right side of the altar. Soon a large cult had grown around it.

St Cuthbert achieved great fame for two reasons, firstly for the great number of miracles performed during and after his lifetime, and secondly, for the fact that his body remained uncorrupt for hundreds of years, as was proved by several inspections over the ages.

When Henry VIII's Commissioners arrived they destroyed his shrine and had the iron bound chest containing St Cuthbert's remains smashed open and broke his left leg in doing so, as there was still a body then still dressed in vestments and with cross and crozier. The last examination took place in 1899, when a skeleton was found with the left shin bone missing.

The Cloisters – Durham Cathedral

In 995 when in danger from Danish raids, the monks with St Cuthbert's body had gone to Ripon. Returning north they reached a place east of Durham where the cart stuck fast. In prayer it was revealed to the monks that St Cuthbert should be enshrined at Dunholme, a hillock in a loop of the river Wear. Here in 1070 a rough shelter was erected, then a wooden church, which stood for three years, and finally the massive stone cathedral was built. The first stones were laid in 1093, and by 1104 a shrine was ready behind the High Altar for St Cuthbert's body. The massive marble slab is just inscribed *Cuthbertus.*

There is a strong tradition that his body was secretly removed to another part of Durham Cathedral. His ring was removed from his finger and is used by the Bishop of Newcastle whenever he ordains a priest.

When the monks fled from Lindisfarne they disinterred St Cuthbert's body, eleven years after his death, and according to Bede 'it was lying on its right side wholly entire and flexible in its joints, and resembled rather a person asleep than one dead.' The monks carried the body about for seven years, reaching Workington at one point, intending to cross the sea to Ireland, but were prevented by severe storms. They also took with them the Lindisfarne Gospels, written in honour of St Cuthbert by Eadfrith,

Venerable Bede's tomb – Durham Cathedral

Bishop from 698 to 721, one of the finest examples of Celtic art. It was in Durham in the 12th century but was 'lost' until the 17th century, when they were in the possession of Parliament. They were then acquired by Sir Robert Cottin and are now in the British Museum.

It was Aidan who came from Iona in 635 and founded his church and monastery on the island of Lindisfarne, from whence he brought the gospel to the whole of Northumbria, and St Cuthbert was the sixth bishop of the See.

St Herbert

A devoted friend of St Cuthbert. He had his cell on an island in Derwentwater, now called St Herbert's Island. A chapel was built there in the 14th century. At one time mass was said on the island once a year on St Herbert's Day, 13th April.

St Kentigern (or St Mungo)

He lived from 518 to 603, and is reputed to be the founder of the Christian Church in Strathclyde, and became bishop of Glasgow. Jocelin, a monk of Furness Abbey, wrote his *Life of St Kentigern* in 1180. Another earlier writing says that he was born at Taneu, daughter of Loth, king of the Lothians. Taneu, saying that she wished to remain a virgin, refused to marry Owain, the son of Urien, king of Rheged, as was her father's wish. He was greatly angered and sent her away to serve a swineherd. Owain visited her in disguise and seduced her. When it was discovered she was with child she was condemned to death and was tied into a chariot and sent hurtling down a hill, Dunpelder, but miraculously survived. She was then put into a coracle, without oars, and pushed out to sea. She came ashore at Culross, Fife, in the Firth of Forth, where her son was born in 518. They were found by shepherds and they told St Servanus, who lived in a nearby monastery. He baptised them both, naming the baby boy 'Kyentyern'. St Servanus kept the boy, and he was brought up by him and the monks. He called the boy 'Munghu' (Mungo), a word of endearment meaning 'dearest friend'.

His mother died in Glasgow, and her bones were venerated. She was known there as St Thenew, and there was a St Thenew's Chapel and St Thenew's Gate. St Thenew's Day was celebrated on the 18th July.

Kentigern and his followers went to Glasgow, where a monastery was built on the site of an ancient Celtic cemetery, consecrated by St Ninian. They supported themselves by rural industry. It is said that St Columba visited him there. Kentigern became bishop of Glasgow. Glasgow took its name from *Glas-cu*, Celtic for 'the church of Kentigern'. Glasgow was originally called *Deschu*.

It is said that after persecution by king Morken of Strathclyde he fled to Wales. He visited Carlisle, and on hearing the need to christianise the peoples in the mountains, proceeded to a place near Derwentwater, where he erected a preaching cross in a clearing in AD 573. This site became known as 'Crosfeld', renamed by the Norse 'Crosthwaite', the cross in the clearing. The present church, 14th century, is dedicated to St Kentigern. Nearby there used to be a 'St Kentigern's Well' at High Hill. In 1506 Dominus Robert Cooke presented to the church a magnificent folio missal, in which is inscribed 'St Kentigern's Day, 12th January'. This is now at Ampleforth School. The coat-of-arms of the nearby Keswick School is associated with St Kentigern.

Many churches in this area of Cumberland are dedicated to St Kentigern or St Mungo, and there are several wells named after him too.

After his death on the 13th January 603, he became, as St Mungo, venerated as Glasgow's patron saint and the Cathedral was built to honour him. He was enshrined in the lower church of the Cathedral, where an altar is dedicated to him.

When the Reformation came all vestiges of St Kentigern were removed from the Cathedral and destroyed and not one item has survived in Scotland. The only known portrait of him is painted on a pillar in the Chapel of St Stephen in Cologne Cathedral.

The coat-of-arms of the City of Glasgow shows the symbols associated with St Kentigern, the bell, the bird, the tree and the fish. The bell is said to have been a gift to the Saint from the Pope. The bird was a dead robin said to have been brought back to life by him when a boy. The tree is said to have rekindled a holy fire which, as a boy, he had let out. The fish is said to have swallowed the Queen's ring in the Clyde, and it was recovered with the help of the Saint.

Kentigern's first church would be of wood. The main church may have been built over his grave. The buildings would have been surrounded by a wall of stone and earth. His grave became a shrine and a place of pilgrimage. The Cathedral was not completed until the 14th century.

Jocelyn of Furness in his *Life of St Kentigern* relates these stories.

St Servanus had several pupils and these were jealous of Kentigern, as he was the favourite. Now St Servanus had a pet robin and one day his pupils were playing with it rather roughly and its head was pulled off. They threw it away and blamed Kentigern for it. When St Servanus heard of the death of the bird he was very angry. Kentigern, however, took the remains of the bird in his hand, putting back the head to the body made the sign of the cross and prayed for its restoration. The robin came to life and flew away to its master.

The pupils in turn had to attend to the lamps in the church and when it came to Kentigern's turn the other boys put out all the lights previously. He however went out and plucked a hazel branch, then prayed and made the sign of the cross over it and breathed upon it. The branch then caught alight and he was able to light all the lamps again.

Their cook died suddenly, and was buried. The others in the community implored St Servanus to ask Kentigern to restore him. The following day the earth was removed and Kentigern prayed over the body, he rose up alive and returned to his duties and lived seven more years.

Another time Kentigern wished to cross a river, and prayed, and the water divided so that he could cross.

In spite of his protests Kentigern was elected as Bishop, in his 25th year, and made his seat in Glasgu (the Dear Family), which extended from sea to sea. He abstained from flesh and wine as much as possible. He wore a rough hair cloth next to his skin and then a goatskin coat over it, and a cowl over his head, then a white alb and a stole over his shoulders, and carried a simple wooden staff, and the manual book. His bed was a hollowed stone with a stone for a pillow. He arose in the very early hours and had prayers and hymns, and then sprang naked into the nearby brook chanting his prayers. During Lent he would depart to a place alone and return before Maundy Thursday and sometimes before Palm Sunday. He would afflict his body on Good Friday, having washed the feet of the poor and lepers. On all his preaching tours he travelled on foot, even in extreme old age. Once when there was a shortage of ploughing oxen, Kentigern by prayer made use of wild stags to plough, and when one was killed by a wolf, by prayer was able to yoke the wolf to the stag, to carry on with the ploughing. Once being short of seed, he used sand and wheat grew in abundance from it.

Once when there was a shortage of grain, and the pagan king's barns were full, he challenged Kentigern to remove the corn without human agency. The Saint prayed, and the river broke its banks and swept the barns away to where Kentigern lived, and deposited them there, dry and undamaged.

After Kentigern's visit to St David, a wild boar led him to a place where he was to build his monastery. After it was built he gathered a large company together including a boy named Asaph. One day in winter he asked Asaph to bring him some live coals to warm himself. Asaph fetched them held in his dress which did not burn. In due course Kentigern made him his successor.

Kentigern went seven times to Rome and brought back many books, relics and ornaments.

King Rederech wrote to Kentigern imploring him to return to his old church at Glasgu. Kentigern who was firmly settled in his monastery prayed long about it when an angel appeared and told him to go back to Glasgu where he was to end his days. Accordingly Kentigern consecrated Asaph as Bishop in his place and left. With him went 365 brethren, leaving 300 in the monastery in Wallia.

King Rederech paid homage to him, and handed over to him the dominance of his kingdom and the king and queen long childless were blessed with a son, due to Kentigern's prayers, and he was baptised and called Constantine and succeeded his father, and subjected himself to the Bishop, and became a great king.

Once when Kentigern was confronted by a great multitude of people he drove out a whole host of devils from them.

Kentigern established many churches and ordained priests and consecrated bishops, building many monasteries and performing many miracles. He was protected from rain, hail and snow.

Once the king's jester, whom he wished to reward, was asked by him what gift he would like, and replied – a dish of mulberries. As it was wintertime the king asked Kentigern to help him, and he told him where he could find some.

St Columba, with a great company, visited Kentigern.

Once some robbers caught one of Kentigern's rams and cut off its head. The ram's body ran back to the flock and fell down. The head immediately turned to stone in the robber's hands and they could not release it. They went to Kentigern and asked for his help and pardon. He enabled them to release their grasp from the stone head, and gave them the carcase, but kept the stone head.

Kentigern ordered a huge stone cross to be made, but when it was completed it was found to be too heavy to move from the quarry. After prayer the cross was miraculously moved to the site in the cemetery. Another cross was made from sea sand and many miracles were performed at its site.

When the time approached for Kentigern to leave this life, an angel appeared to him and told him to take a warm bath the following day when he would fall asleep in it and be taken to the Lord, and any of his disciples could do the same, and go in spirit with him, and this came to pass. Kentigern's body was laid under a stone on the right side of the altar. He was 185 years old.

The Bishopric extended from the Clyde to the Solway Firth, from the western boundary of Lothian to the River Urr on the west. The erection of the Cathedral was begun by David before 1124, and dedicated on the 7th July 1136. King David liberally endowed the church. It was built in stone in the Norman style.

Little was known about the early church until the beginning of the 12th century, when Earl David, Prince of Cumbria, appointed an Inquest to find out the early possessions of St Kentigern's church, and the result is in the Notitia, the first document of the Register of the Bishopric, which he reconstituted.

The relics of St Constantine were in the church at Govan, which is dedicated to the Saint. It is thought that due to Viking raids, they were moved upstream to a new site for a monastery on the south bank of the Clyde, opposite the River Kelvin.

In the 6th and 7th centuries the Celtic church expanded through Strathclyde. Troubled times were to follow due to invasions and raids. In 780 Dumbarton was burned, and sacked in 875 and 945. The kingdom was then invaded by Edmund of Wessex, who ceded it to Malcolm, king of the Scots. Stratchclyde became independent and remained so until the death of Owain in 1018, when it was joined with the Scottish kingdom. By the 12th century the diocese of Glasgow included most of Cumberland and Westmorland.

King David reigned from 1124 to 1153. He appointed his former teacher John as first bishop, and he died in 1147. He granted to the bishop the church of Renfrew, Govan and its church, the church of Cadihon, the tithe of his kain in Strathgrif, Cuningham, Kyle and Carrick, and the eighth penny of all the pleas of Court throughout Cumbria and the church of Lockorwort. The Cathedral Church was destroyed by fire before 1189. The new Cathedral was dedicated on the 6th July 1197. It came under the jurisdiction of the See of Rome, and not the Archbishop of York.

15

Ireland

About 500 BC Celts arrived from the Rhine via Scotland. In the following centuries La Tène metal work appeared in Ireland. By the first century BC there was a strong Celtic society there. The pagan Celtic period lasted until about 450 AD. Most of the decorated metalwork and carved stone which bears early La Tène art is found north of a line drawn between the cities of Dublin and Galway. The major royal centres were also in the northern half of the country, Tara, Co. Meath, Navan Fort, Co. Armagh and Rathcroghan, Co. Roscammon. After the introduction of Christianity in the 5th century the whole island shared the same language, legal system, social organisation and material culture.

The first period, 300 BC to 100 AD was that in which the La

Newgrange, Co. Meath

Newgrange, Co. Meath (interior)

Tène culture was introduced and consolidated. This new art was a
highly sophisticated abstract style of curvilinear ornamentation,
heavily illustrated by classical vegetal motifs, such as the vine,
palm and lotus, and by oriental animal art, which was used on
weapons and ornaments. Irish art developed a distinctive
character.

Society was ruled over by a warrior aristocracy. It was an
agricultural society in which wealth was measured in terms of
cattle. The descendants of Niall dominated the midlands and mid
and west Ulster, and assumed the kingship of Tara. In Munster
the Eoganachta controlled the kingship of Cashel. The Ulaid of
east Ulster, the Lagin of Leinster and the Connachta did not
accept the new order, and resisted efforts to subject them.

Lake dwellings, known as *crannógs*, came into use, as well as
enclosed settlements, known as 'raths' or ringforts. The *crannógs*
were built over water on a raised platform, and surrounded by a
circular palisade, with a wooden footbridge to the bank.

In the first centuries AD Ireland was divided into four large
kingdoms, Ulaid (Ulster), Connachta (Connacht), Laigin (Leinster)

94

Staighe Fort – Co. Kerry

and Mumn (Munster). Ulster was ruled by Conchobar macNessa, and Connacht by Queen Medb.

Later at Tara, in Meath, a new dynasty was founded by Niall Noigiallach (379 AD). His descendants annexed Ulster in the 5th century. From 506 to 1036 the north of Ireland was divided between the two kingdoms of Ui Neill, based at Ailech, and the southern kingdom of Ui Neill, based at Tara.

The southern half of Ireland was more culturally advanced than the north. The constant conflict between Ui Neill and Leinster weakened the latter, and Munster became the dominant kingdom in the south, with the royal capital at Cashel, in Tipperary. Here the cultural life of Ireland blossomed. By the early Christian period there were seven kingdoms, three new ones having been formed out of Ulster. The two High Kings in control were the Eoganachta of Munster in the south, and the Ui Neill in the north.

In Ireland there were only very small tribal concentrations and it remained a rural country. Women enjoyed rights almost similar to men, and in the royal family could accede to the monarchy, as happened with Boudicca and Cortismandua. Tara Hill, Co. Meath, was a royal settlement, and the residence of the High King, as well as a meeting place.

In Irish law the annual rent for six cows was a calf, a salted pig, three sacks of malt, half a sack of wheat and a handful of rush candles. In law the family consisted of four generations.

In the 4th century, when the Romans were in decline in Britain, Irish and other barbarian tribes began to invade Britain. Scottii from Dalriada (Co. Antrim) invaded Scotland and set up an Irish colony, centred at Dunadd. The Irish also colonised Pembroke, South Wales, Dyfed and the Isle of Man.

Contact with Rome had brought Christianity to Ireland. In 431 AD Pope Celestine sent Palladius as bishop to the Irish believing in Christ. He died in 461.

In 433 St Patrick lit a light on the Hill of Slane, as a sign of the new religion he was preaching, Christianity. Although he did not succeed in converting the High King Laoghaire, he did succeed in converting almost the whole of the country within his lifetime. Wooden churches were in use for a long period before stone ones were built.

About 500 his church was organised to become based on monasticism, ruled by abbots whose jurisdiction extended over the

Irish Celtic cross

surrounding areas. Throughout the 6th century the monastic movement made great strides and laid the foundations of great centres of culture, which fostered writing, especially the making of illuminated manuscripts and books, for example, the Book of Durrow in the 7th century and the *Book of Kells* in the 8th and 9th centuries.

Many of the old Celtic tales which had been kept intact orally for centuries, were at last written down and preserved. The copying of manuscripts was an essential part of Christian monastic life, which had been brought over from Roman Britain. Gospels were necessary for study, and for the liturgical needs of the new churches, as well as the missionary work of the Irish monks. Latin was used, through the translation of the *Vulgate*, as commissioned by Pope Damasus, from St Jerome, in the 4th century, and both pocket editions as well as large luxury ones were produced. Some books became regarded as sacred relics and were used as a cure for both sick animals and humans. Irish book shrines were made to enclose and protect manuscripts, as covers were unknown.

Croziers were the most common form of reliquary, as they were believed to contain the staffs of the early saints and as such to have the power to work miracles.

Irish monks went to Whithorn, and to St David's in Wales, to study and learn about asceticism. On returning home they set up cells in isolated places. At Kildare a community of monks and nuns was founded by St Brigid.

The monastery of Nendrum on Rahee Island. Co. Down, was founded in the 5th century, it is thought by St Mochnoi. On the site of the monastery of Reask a number of decorated stone slabs have been found, dated 7th/8th century. In Ballinderry a 9th century metal hanging lamp, and a Manx 10th century square wooden gaming board with 49 holes were found during excavation work by the Harvard Mission.

Christianity blossomed between the 5th and 12th centuries, when many beautiful items were produced in the monasteries, such as the Ardagh Chalice, and the Tara Brooch, as well as many High Crosses, and liturgical vessels, vestments, books and sculptures. The earliest stone carvings were stone slabs with simple incised crosses. Sometimes the ringed Celtic cross was used.

The Irish Church carried Christianity to North-West Europe and Britain and helped to spread it and keep it alive. This was the work of monks from many different monasteries. Irish monks from Ireland and Iona sailed to the Hebrides, and reached the Orkneys and Shetland, and Iceland. By the 7th century they had penetrated the whole of the British Isles. They also reached Gaul, the Rhineland, Switzerland and Italy. St Brendan of Clonfert, the wide travelled Irish abbot of the 6th century, used a coracle, and visited St Columba on Iona. He wrote, in Latin, the *Navigatio*, which also described the construction of a coracle. He constructed a special coracle using oxhide over a wooden frame and voyaged in it to America and back. He was abbot of Llancarvan, and tutored St Malo of Brittany. The most important Celtic monasteries were Bobbio in Italy, Luxuel in Gaul and Bangor in Ireland.

The entire crown of the monk's head was shaven and no fringe was left above the forehead.

The Ogam alphabet was invented by Irish monks in SW Ireland about the 4th century AD, based on the Latin alphabet. It was only used for funerary epitaphs. It was taken to Scotland by Irish colonists in the 5th century. It has 20 letters made up of one to five strokes cut at varying angles on the edge of a stone.

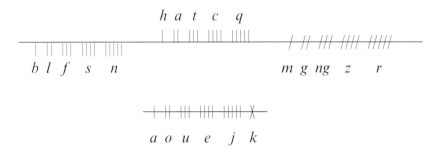

Irish society was composed of a great number of small farmers, and petty kings, responsible to the High King of Tara, and it was their love of independence that prevented any kind of united front against aggression. Limited trade in luxury goods was carried on but most of the better off homesteads were self-sufficient. Kinship was important in defining legal positions of peoples as the land was often owned by kin-groups, and not by individuals. The country was divided into many petty tribal kingdoms, called *tuatha*, ruled by kings who were both war leaders and judges, and who had sacral functions. Jurists, *Crehons*, were the guardians of the law, while learned men, *Filé*, were both poets and seers. The best craftsmen held a high status.

The monastic communities functioned like the kin-groups. Many early monasteries developed on sites of isolated hermitages. This led to the reclamation of marginal lands, especially in the midland areas. Many monasteries became wealthy and powerful, and the office of Abbot became to be regarded as hereditary. Irish monasteries received large numbers of foreign students, including Saxons and Northumbrians. These contacts proved a great benefit to Irish civilisation and their effects can be noticed in metalwork, manuscripts and sculpture.

As need for missionary work declined in the late 7th and 8th centuries, Irish monks continued going abroad on pilgrimages, and some remained in the churches and courts of Western Europe.

When the Vikings invented the keel boat about 600 AD they were able to undertake long sea voyages. They settled in England and the Scottish Isles, Sicily and Normandy, and they reached the Faroes, Iceland, Greenland and America. They first raided Ireland in 795, and the raids continued for another half century before they made their first settlement. The Vikings made the Abbeys and monasteries their prime target for plunder and huge quantities of gold and silver and manuscripts and books were looted, a great loss to the churches. Until they arrived in Ireland there were no towns, and the Vikings built the first ones, commencing with Dublin in 841. Wexford, Waterford, Cork and Limerick followed in the next century.

These towns became important trading centres, especially Dublin, and markets were established. The Vikings of Dublin minted the first money in Ireland about 997.

In the old city of Dublin over 100,000 Viking objects have been found during excavations.

The Irish king Maelschechnaill defeated the Dublin Vikings in the battle of Tara in 980. 34 years later they were again defeated by king Brian Boru. After this peace reigned, and the Vikings settled down as traders. However, in 1014 at the battle of Clontarf they were finally defeated by the Irish. After the end of the 10th century they began to intermarry.

Following the Norman invasion of Ireland in 1170, king Henry II visited Dublin in 1171/72 and gave the city to the men of Bristol to colonise. Dublin Castle was built.

Within 30 years the Normans had conquered a large part of the eastern area and fortified it by building mottes, mounds on which they erected a wooden tower, a *bretesche*. At the foot of the motte they had a bailey where horses and cattle were kept. They did not start to build stone castles until about 1200, the largest being Trim, in Co. Meath. About 40 have survived. About 80 Round Towers have also survived. They were used by the monks as bell towers and places of refuge, and date back to the early 10th century, and were usually built as part of the monastery complex. The Norman invasion reached its peak in 1235.

About 3,000 castles and tower houses were built by the Normans and Irish from 1150 to 1600.

In the later Middle Ages many churches, abbeys and friaries

were built. The Cistercian Order was the most influential. Malachy, bishop of Armagh, visited the Cistercians in Clairvaux in 1139, and left behind some of his followers to train in the Order. He was granted some land by the king of Airghigela in Co. Louth on the River Mattock, and there founded the first Irish Cistercian Abbey in 1142, and called it Mellifont. His followers returned from Clairvaux and formed the first community. St Malachy died in 1148 on a journey to Rome. Mellifont was consecrated in 1157. This abbey was destroyed, and a second one built about 1315.

The introduction of the Cistercian Order to the Irish monastic life brought an important new impetus which lasted until the Reformation in 1536, 37 other Cistercian houses being founded. These were supplemented by other new orders, the Augustinians, Benedictines, Dominicans and Franciscans. During the period of the Reformation, the monks and laity struggled to retain their religion and independence.

Celtic Religious Art

By the mid to late 6th century the earliest Irish manuscript, the Cathach of St Columba, a psalter, appeared. It had simple coloured decorations.

The Book of Kells

It was written about 800 AD in majuscule script in 340 folios. It contains the four Gospels in a Latin text based on the Vulgate, intermixed with readings from the old Latin translation. The gospels are preceded by prefaces, summaries of the narrative and Eusabian canon tables. There are 678 illuminated pages and two without. Originally it was kept within a golden cover. It is Celtic art at its best.

In the 12th century charters in Irish, relating to the Monastery of Kells, were copied into hitherto blank pages. It was first mentioned in 1007 when the Annals of Ulster record its theft from the church of Kells, and its subsequent recovery 'under a sod'.

It is possible that the Book was produced on Iona, for when the Vikings attacked the monastery there in 806, and killed 68 members of the community, most of the remaining monks moved to Kells and settled there by 814. Some of the leaves were lost in

1007. In the 12th century the Columban monastery at Kells was dissolved, but the Book remained there in what now became the Parish Church. During the Cromwellian invasion in 1654 the Book was sent to Dublin and in 1661 the bishop of Meath presented it to Trinity College, Dublin, where it still is. It is beautifully decorated.

The village of Kells, in Co. Kilkenny, was in the ancient kingdom of Ossory. In the 5th century, St Kieran of Seir, the patron saint of the Ossory diocese, founded a monastery there, of which very little now remains. After the Norman invasion it was granted to Geoffrey FitzRobert de Monte Marisco, a Norman knight. He strengthened and refortified the position in 1192, and later he built a castle on the site. In 1183, he founded a priory a mile away, dedicated to St Mary. The monks, of the Augustinian Order, were brought over from Bodmin, Cornwall, and Hugh de Rous was appointed the first English bishop of Ossory.

The new priory was fortified, with six dwelling towers. In 1252 William de Bermingham captured and fired the town of Kells, and in 1316 Edward Bruce captured it. A few years later the de Berminghams returned. Arnold Le Poer inherited the town, but it was again captured and fired by the Earl of Desmond. In 1346 the de Berminghams were granted the Manor of Kells. In the 16th century it came into the hands of the Butlers of Mountgarret and it remained in their possession until they were dispossessed by Cromwell in 1650.

In 1540 the Priory had been suppressed by Henry VIII. The estate of 352 hectacres, a grange, two castles, three water mills and eel weirs, many cottages, and an interest in 24 rectories in various counties, was dispersed, while the Priory was granted to John Butler, Earl of Ormond.

Kells Priory covered about five acres and was the largest monastic institution in Ireland. The large, oblong area used by the foundation was divided into two courts by a wall and moat. The fortified north court was defended by towers as well as by a wall, and contained some of the most important buildings, the church and cloisters. A strong castle built on the south-east angle of the choir is said to have been the prior's quarters. The priory is now only ruins.

St Brigid of Kildare founded a monastery at Kilree, about two miles from Kells. There is a Brigidine Well, and a stone said to have the imprint of St Brigid's knees, *Glun Brighde*, a round tower and a fine carved wheel High Cross. Kilree is thought to be the burial place of Niall Caille MacAeda, High King of Ireland, who died 846.

Book of Armagh

This was written in 807, in monuscale script. It is the only surviving early Irish manuscript with a complete New Testament. Included are canon tables, prefaces and interpretations of Hebrew names. Also with it is St Patrick's confession, two 7th century accounts of his life, and the life of St Martin of Tours by Sulpicius Severus.

It was made by Ferdomnach for Torbach, who was the Abbot of Armagh in 807. It was in charge of a hereditary keeper in the Middle Ages and then in the 17th century passed to the Brownlow family of Lurgan. It was bought from them by the Archbishop of Armagh for the library of Trinity College, Dublin. There is little use of colour.

Book of Dimma

It was written in the late 8th century, in minuscule script. It contains the four Gospels in the old Latin translation from the *Vulgate*, also with the late 10th and early 11th centuries Service for visiting the sick. It was attributed to the work of the scribe Dimma, probably in the monastery of Roscrea, Co. Tipperary, and probably for Dionchride. It remained obscure until 1836, when Sir William Betham sold it to Trinity College, Dublin. Its decorations are not of a very high standard.

Book of Durrow

This was written about 675, in majuscule script. There are four Gospels in Latin, Eusbian canon tables, Jerome's letter to Pope Damasus, prefaces summaries and glossaries of Hebrew names. It was probably produced in Durrow monastery, Co. Offaly, which was founded by St Columba in 553. It is close to the *Vulgate*. It remained at Durrow until the monastery was dissolved in the 16th century. In 1661 the bishop presented it to Trinity College, Dublin.

The Book is decorated with framed symbols, carpet pages and the illumination of the opening words.

Stowe Missal

It was written about 800, in nunuscule and angular script. A Latin mass book of the early Irish Church. Probably written in Tallaght, Co. Dublin, as the abbot of the priory, St Máel Ruain, who died 792, is commemorated in the Mass. In about 1050 it was in Lorrha, Co. Tipperary. In the 19th century it was in the Duke of Buckingham's collection at his Stowe House. It was bought by the British Government and presented in 1883 to the Royal Irish Academy, Dublin. It is bound in oak boards covered by vellum, and consists of two separate manuscripts. The first is the St John's Gospel in 11 folios. The second Missal in 56 folios contains the Ordinary and Canon of the Mass, the Order of Baptism, the Order of Visitation of the Sick, of Extreme Unction and Communion. There is also an Irish Tract on the Mass, Irish spells against injury to the eye, and disease of the urine. Except for one page it is not decorated.

Celtic Treasure

The Broighter Hoard

The most magnificent hoard of gold objects to have been found in Ireland was unearthed by a plough at Broighter, Co. Derry, in 1896. Of the seven items found, five were neck ornaments, torcs, the most sumptuous of which is a large gold collar, of Irish La Tène outstanding craftsmanship. Its raised decoration is based on classical foliage designs. The hinge is missing. Two other torcs, one incomplete, are made of twisted gold bars. There were two gold neck chains, probably Roman. There was also a small bowl and the model of a ship. They were probably buried in the 1st century BC.

The Petrie Crown

This is probably 2nd century AD. Remains of two sets of Celtic headgear have been found, one in Cork, known as the 'Cork

Horns', and the other, place of discovery unknown, known as the 'Petrie Crown', after the name of the person in whose collection it once was.

It is made of thin cast bronze, and is held together by rivets and solder. It is decorated with curved designs ending in bird's heads. There have been red enamel studs. It would have been attached to a leather or cloth cap, and would have been worn by a person of rank.

Hoards of Roman silver were found at Balline, Co. Limerick and Ballinrees, Co. Derry. These were probably booty brought back from raids on Britain. A bronze trumpet with La Tène decorations on the mouth ring was found at Loughnashade, Co. Armagh. A gold tubular torc with buffer terminals was found. A gold ribbon torc and decorated box were found at Somerset, Co. Galway, of 1st century AD date. A hoard from Attymon, Co. Galway, consisted of two bridle bits, and a pair of Y-shaped bronzes. Large decorated bronze discs off chariots, were found at Monasterevin, 1st or 2nd century AD. There are some standing stones in La Tène style, the earliest are at Turoe, Co. Galway, of 3rd century BC. A decorated stone was at Mullaghmast, Co. Kildare, of 6th century AD. There are also undecorated stones, as the 'Stone of Destiny' at Tara. Stone heads of Celtic Gods have also been found. A three-faced head was at Corleck, Co. Cavan. A wooden idol of yew was found in a bog at Ralaghan, Co. Cavan. (The yew was sacred.) A Penannular brooch was found at Ballinderry crannog, Co. Offaly, of 7th century AD date.

Two of the finest cliff forts are Dun Aoughus on Inishmore, Aran Islands, and Dun Kilmore on Achillbeg, Co. Mayo.

Glendalough, Co. Wicklow, was chosen for a hermitage by St Kevin in the 6th century. It soon developed into an important settlement and place of pilgrimage. It was raided by the Vikings in the 9th and 10th centuries and was damaged by floods in 1174. The 103 ft Round Tower is well preserved, the conical roof having been reconstructed.

Muireadach's Cross, Monasterboice, Co. Louth, was a monastic settlement to St Buithe in the 5th century. This cross is the finest of a group of crosses, and thought to be erected by a 10th century abbot. It is 17 ft 8 ins high and very richly decorated with scriptural themes. Nearby are the ruins of two minor churches, and the remains of a Round Tower still 100 ft high.

Monasterboice High Cross, Co. Louth

The mountain, Croaghpatrick, Co. Mayo, takes its name from St Patrick, who it is said fasted on its summit for 40 days in 441. Today, an annual pilgrimage takes place in July, when tens of thousands of people climb to the top of the 2,510 ft mountain, where there is a modern chapel. Some go barefoot, making stations at the holy mounds on the ascent.

The Rock of Cashel, Co. Tipperary. On the top of a massive limestone outcrop stands the great church and fort. It was held for seven centuries by the kings of Cashel and Munster. It was founded in the 4th century. St Patrick baptised the king of Cashel in 450. In 1101 Muirchertach O'Brien granted the Rock to the church and it became the See of Munster. The church was built between 1127/34. The 13th century Gothic Cathedral supplanted an old church built 1169 by Donal Mor O'Brien. There was a 10th century Round Tower, the ruin of a high castle and a High Cross.

Ardmore Round Tower, Co. Waterford, is 95 ft high. It is associated with St Declan and became a place of pilgrimage. Next to the tower are the ruins of St Declan's church, the site of a monastic settlement, 10th to the 14th centuries. There is a Declan's

Cashel, Co. Tipperary

Holy Well and Stone and a hermitage church near the cliff, called Temple Disert.

There were simple pit graves and more elaborate ones. Cremation was normally practised. Glass beads and brooches have been found in graves. Roman coins and pottery have been found indicating either trading or booty from raids.

In the 8th and 9th centuries new techniques in metal working enabled the adoption of colours in jewellery in the form of enamels. Later amber studs were used. Highly decorative brooches were produced and they were very popular. Massive silver ornaments were made for the Vikings. St Patrick's companion, St Assicus, was a highly-skilled bronzesmith, who produced many articles for churches.

There were Bardic schools in Ireland until the 17th century. The pupils had to undergo a 12-year apprenticeship.

Galway

Galway City, which gave its name to the surrounding area, was originally a Norman settlement. It is western Ireland's principal city and its name derives from the river.

Clonmachoise

Clonmachoise

The village and its fort were part of the O'Halloran territories, but were seized by the Norman de Burgos, who built a castle there prior to 1240. It was later walled and fortified. Richard II granted it a charter in 1484, which made it independent. It was ruled mainly by Norman and Welsh families. The dispossessed du Burgos harassed it and then the O'Flaherties. It had a famous classical school with 1,200 students, but it was suppressed by Cromwell, when he captured the city after a nine months' siege in 1652. The Williamite wars at the end of the 17th century resulted in another siege.

It became an administration centre in the 18th and 19th centuries.

The Act of Union in 1800 brought Ireland under the control of the British Parliament and it became increasingly necessary to use English. This and the famines of 1845 to 1848 brought disaster to Galway. This resulted in massive emigrations to America and other countries for several generations, leading to depopulation. Between 1841 and 1860 about 1.75 million Irish left the country, between 1861 and 1900 about two million left and a decreasing number until 1940. In all, about five million migrated to the USA during this period.

Queen's College (now University College) was founded in 1846 and a rail link to Dublin came in 1854. Emigration continued throughout the 1880s. In 1890 the British Government established the Congested Districts' Board, to promote traditional crafts and industries in the poorer parts of western Ireland and for 30 years did much valuable work. In 1896 the first regular steamer service between Galway and the Aran Islands was established by the Board and they also helped with the development of modern sea fishing and kelp processing.

Galway County Council was established in 1898 and by the end of the 19th century Galway and the west of Ireland re-awakened to its Celtic past, particularly after the founding of the Gaelic League (*Conradh na Gaeilge*) in 1893. This was followed by the emergence of eminent writers, such as Synge, Yeats, O'Casey and Joyce.

However, it was not until the establishment of the Irish State in 1922 that Galway began to grow and expand. After the 1929 University Act, Galway College of the National University became a centre of bilingual higher education, while a state sponsored Irish Theatre (*Taibhdheare na Gaillimhe*) was founded.

In 1969 the Congested District's Board's successor, *Gaeltarra Eireann*, moved its headquarters from Dublin to Na Forbacha, on the Cois Tharraige coast, 11 km west of the city, whilst the Department responsible for the Irish-speaking areas (*Roinn na Gaeltachta*) was moved nearby in 1975. This was replaced in 1980 by *Údarána Gaeltachta*.

Galway Corporation and the Office of Mayor were abolished in 1840, but were restored in 1937. In 1967 the Industrial Development Authority began a major industrial estate on the east side of Galway City, at Mervue, and leading multi-national firms have established themselves there. In 1972 Galway Regional Technical College was opened, specialising in hotel and catering studies. In

110

1972 the headquarters of *Radio na Gaeltachta* was established at Casla, 32 km west of Galway.

A major fishing harbour is being developed at Ros an Mhil, on the north coast of Galway Bay, and Carnmore Airport, 8 km east of the city is being expanded.

The *Gaeltacht*

An *Gaeltacht* is the name given to those communities in Ireland where the Irish language is in general use and where the old cultural traditions are preserved and promoted. Ireland was an Irish-speaking country to the 16th century, but pressure from the English Government, and the rise of an English speaking commercial class in the 18th century, the founding of Maynooth College in 1795, where clergy were trained, instead of on the continent, the Act of Union with Britain in 1800, the founding of the National School system in 1831, which was structured to favour the superiority of English, and the famine of the 1840s, all helped to erode the Irish language and culture to a disastrous degree. The census of 1851 recorded that Irish was spoken by only a quarter of the population. By 1911 it was just an eighth.

In 1893 the Gaelic League (*Conradh na Gaeilge*) was founded by Dr Douglas Hyde, and this finally led to the establishment of the Irish Free State in 1922. The new state was committed to an Irish revival, which included the strengthening of the *Gaeltacht* communities, with their language, culture and literary heritage. These communities are generally bilingual, English being their second language.

The Galway *Gaeltacht* comprise the three Aran Islands, the Iar-Chonnachta area along the north coast of Galway Bay to Carna, and the areas of north Connemara, the Joyce country, west of Lough Corrib into south Mayo. These communities have been brought closer together by the establishment of *Radio na Gaeltachta* and by the Irish summer colleges which were established at the turn of the century.

The new Irish State restored Irish to all school curricula. At the beginning of the century Iar-Chonnachta and Aran were principal sources of the intellectual and literary movement which resulted in the Irish War of Independence 1916 to 21.

Courses in Irish language are held in various centres throughout the Gaeltacht in the months of June, July and August. In all cases students stay in the homes of local people. Classes are held in the mornings and recreation in the afternoons. At night there are Céill dancing and musical entertainment. Government support to these courses ensure that they are reasonably priced. *Rouin na Gaeltachta* has a list of approved accommodation.

The *Gaeltacht* areas qualify for special concessions in relation to public and local government services. Grants for housing, education and home industries, etc. are obtainable. These areas are in some of Ireland's most beautiful counties, situated in most cases along a rugged, spectacular coastline, Donegal, Mayo, Galway, Kerry, Cork and Waterford.

The Donegal *Gaeltacht* contains the largest Irish-speaking population and stretches from Fanad Head to Kilcar. St Gweedore is an all-Irish theatre and the Donegal *Radio na Gaeltachta* studios. There are a number of islands, including Tory and Arranmore.

In the Kerry area of Slea Head, beehive stone cells built by monks can still be seen. Near Bellyferriter is the 6th century Gallarus Oratory.

In the Cork area there is Gougane Barra where St Finbar founded his monastery, and in Ballingeary the first Irish college was founded in 1904.

The airline *Aer Araun* was established in 1970 to operate regular services between Galway and the Aran Islands.

Due to movements in the rural population many of the islands off the west coast have become abandoned, which has been a great loss to the *Gaeltacht*.

The National Folk Theatre of Ireland (*Siamsa tíre*) is situated at Godfrey Place, Tralee.

Archaeological Excavations

The first extensive survey of ancient monuments was made by George Petrie between 1833 and 1839, when he was working for the Historical Commission of Ireland's first Ordnance Survey. His work on Tara, the Round Towers and the early ecclesiastical architecture was published in 1838 and 1845 and was the foundation of Irish Archaeology.

In 1849 the Kilpenny Archaeological Society was founded, and this later became the Royal Society of Antiquaries of Ireland.

In the 19th century the Royal Irish Academy gathered together a large collection of antiquaries, many of which are now in the National Museum of Ireland, Dublin.

In the 1890s George Coffey, Curator of Antiquaries in the National Museum began scientific excavations. He was followed by R. A. S. Macalister, who became in 1909 the first Professor of Archaeology in the National University of Ireland and for the next 35 years carried out many excavations. Similar work was carried out by Thomas Johnson Westropp from 1890 to 1922. From 1932 Estyn Evans and Oliver Davies began exploring megalithic tombs.

In 1932 the Harvard University Archaeological Mission arrived and under the leadership of Hallam J. Movius and Hugh Hencken carried out important excavations at Poulawack and Ballinderry.

Later important excavating work was carried on by G. F. Mitchell, Séan P. O'Riordáin, Joseph Raftery and M. J. O'Kelly.

Every year between 30 and 40 excavations are carried out and these are reported in *Excavation*, the publication of the Association of Young Irish Archaeologists.

Ireland because of its isolation was probably the last country in Europe to be colonised by man.

In 1928 John Kaye Charlesworth suggested that the caves along the south coast should be examined for traces of early man. E. K. Tratman directed the work in Co. Waterford and settled upon Kilgreavy Cave. Hearths from prehistoric man were found, of Bronze or Iron Age, and Neolithic or Late Stone Age. A polished stone axe was found, also the skull and bones of a female, and another skeleton on the same level as the lowest hearth, together with bones of Ice Age animals. This was an indication that man existed whilst most of Ireland was under glaciers. However, Hallam J. Movius carried on Tratman's work in the Kilgreavy Cave and investigated it to a much greater depth and came to the conclusion that the skeletons were of the Neolithic period, so the age of first man in Ireland remains unsolved, although about 6,800 BC there is evidence of man being there. It was thought that he would cross over from Scotland to NE Ireland.

Early Bronze Age man arrived in Ireland about 2,000 BC. They knew about metals, panned for gold in the rivers and made beautiful ornaments with it, first using thin sheet gold. As supplies of gold increased they made heavier solid gold ornaments. Some of their copper mines remain intact today in west Cork. They obtained the ore by lighting fires in the mine and heating the rock, then poured water over it to make it crack, when the ore was loosened by hammering with cobbles, either held by hand or with rope handles. They produced bronze by using a mixture of 90% copper and 10% tin. Iron appeared about the 6th century BC, but they continued to use bronze.

About 50 hillforts and 30,000 ringforts are known to exist. The ringforts were not forts in reality, but small settlements within circular earthen banks and ditches. It is thought they were generally built after 400 AD. Some were still in use up to the 17th century. The finest example is at Staigue, Co. Kerry. The Turoe Stone, found outside the Rath of Feerwore, is decorated in the Celtic La Tène style in curvilinear pattern, dated after 300 BC.

The Irish National Museum, Dublin

A large variety of Celtic artefacts are housed in the Museum, which have either been found accidentally or during excavations. These include stone hammers and axes, food vessels and cups, gold collars and earrings, armlets, dress fasteners, round boxes, pins, bronze swords and shields, spearheads, cauldrons, horns, trumpets and brooches. There are also bronze and silver chalices, bells and buckets. Carved stone and wooden objects, shrines, croziers, crosses and several hoards.

In 1842 Thomas Davis co-founded the weekly *The Nation*, which was devoted solely to the cause of Irish National freedom.

The Easter Monday rising in Dublin on the 24th April 1916, led by Patrick Henry Pearse, only lasted a few days, was promptly suppressed by the British Army and Navy and the leaders executed by firing squad.

In the General Election of December 1918 Sinn Fean won 73 of the 105 Irish seats, but did not sit in Westminster, but set up its own Republican Party, the Dail Eireann, which ratified the Republic proclaimed in 1916. Its first objective was the expulsion of the English Garrison. The next 2½ years guerrilla warfare was pursued with the aid of the IRA, and there was widespread revolt. After long negotiations in 1921, the Anglo-Irish Treaty was signed in 1922, and the Irish Free State came into being in the south.

However a period of civil war ensued until May 1923 before Eire was founded.

The Constitution of Ireland was enacted on the 1st July 1937.

'Article 2. (*Airteagal* 2)
The national territory consists of the whole Island of Ireland, its islands and the territorial seas.'
'*Is é oileán na hEireann go heomláu, maille lena oileáin agus a fharraigé teoraun, na oríocha náisiínta.*'

Irish is the official language of the 26 county Republic, with English as the second language. It has a population of almost three million.

A democratic form of elected government was chosen, with a President, as Head of State. The Prime Minister (in Irish, *Taoiseach*, Chieftain, and the Deputy, *Tanaiste*). The House of Parliament, *Dail*, the ancient Celtic meeting place. This was a complete break from the long-established Celtic tribal system.

In the GPO in Dublin, from where the rebellion took place in 1916 is a statue of the dying Cuchalaiun, the great Celtic hero, with the raven on his shoulder.

The Great Blasket, the largest of a group of small islands off the south-west coast of Ireland, was once the home of a small thriving Gaelic-speaking fishing community, but is now deserted.

The community was based on kinship and co-operation, and during the last half century of its existence members of it produced more than a dozen books, several of which have been translated into English, and one *Twenty Years A-Growing* has been world famous. These books give a picture of the life of the community as it was.

It is not known how long the Blasket Islands were inhabited. Of all the Gaelic languages Irish is the most archaic, and contains some features that seem to stem from pre-Celtic languages long disappeared. It is exceptionally rich in folk tales, of which there are three categories. First, are the heroic tales, which include the Ulster Cycle. Secondly, are the tales of local history and, thirdly, are the religious, magical and romantic tales. These tales show no distinction between the natural and supernatural. The natural world was believed to be peopled by hostile forces, which could only be kept at bay by heroic deeds and faith in God. The people knew these tales well and loved them and introduced them to their children from an early age. Some excelled in the art of story telling, carrying on the Celtic tradition in this respect.

Peig Sayers in her book *Peig*, recalls that her father was an outstanding storyteller, even to the very end of his long life of 96 years and that the village boys used to gather in his house to hear them.

The Irish tribal system collapsed under the impact of the Cromwellian and Williamite wars and Ireland became an English Colony and subject to English laws. The Catholics were denied political rights and were forbidden to practice their religion and had to send their children abroad to educate them. As only English was used in administration and in commerce, the Irish language went into a decline and eventually fell to the level of a patois and the majority of Irish people became English speaking, although many in the rural areas became bilingual, which led to an English dialect. Only the most remote and isolated areas retained their Gaelic language.

After the founding of the Gaelic League in 1885 the revival of the Irish language began, as also did Irish scholarship. Old and middle Irish were already subjects of study in Dublin, and in several Continental universities, and today this is being carried on in the Universities of Bonn and Innsbruck. Foreign scholars were attracted to the Irish Gaelic communities, especially the Blasket Islands, to learn their language and dialects and folktales. Robin Flower visited them in 1910, and recorded many tales from Tomás ó Crohan which were published in 1956. The journal of the latter was published in Gaelic in 1928, as *Island Arguments*. His autobiography *The Islandmen*, was published in 1929. Maurice O'Sullivan wrote *Twenty Years A-Growing*. Peig Sayers' son, Mícheál O'Guheen, wrote three books. Other autobiographies, a phrase book of the local dialect, poetry and others, were produced, making in all 17 volumes. Besides these were songs of praise, hymns, wedding songs, laments, elegies, satires, lampoons, etc.

In earlier times poets were attached to the clan courts, but after the battle of Aughrim in 1691, the Clan Chiefs fled the country, and the poets and scholars were dispersed amongst the peasants, and helped to educate their children in defiance of the law.

Further books written about the Blasket Islanders were, *An Old*

Woman's Reflections by Peig Sayers, in 1962 and 1978, *The Irish Tradition* by Robin Flower in 1947, and *The Western Isles*, also by him, in 1978, and *Early Celtic Poetry* by K. Jackson, in 1936.

In an article in the *Evening Echo*, Cork, on the 24th February 1988, written by Michael Dromey, he writes about the 'New Irish Language Schools'. Pádraig O'Cuanachaen, Cultural and Language Development Officer for the Munster *Gaeltachta*, has for the past four years been engaged in the setting up of *Gaelscoileanna* throughout Munster and had led an enthusiastic movement that had seen the establishment of 18 all-Irish schools in Munster. It has brought the Irish language to the masses of the people. These people welcomed it and appreciated it and many were prepared to make considerable sacrifices to have their children educated through it. The whole scheme cost £105,000.

Pádraig sums up, 'All the problems of the past few years have left me with a sense of great hope and a great respect for and confidence in the ordinary Irish people. I have more hope now than ever for the restoration of the Irish language.

The Institute of Irish Studies was established on the 1st October 1988 at Liverpool University and not only provides Irish Studies courses for both undergraduates and postgraduates but it will also act as a resource and co-ordination centre for Irish Studies at all levels throughout Britain.

Meanwhile, the British Association for Irish Studies, under whose aegis the Liverpool development has come about, is to have a permanent secretariat, and will launch a fund-raising programme. BAIS, which was founded at a conference at St Peter's College, Oxford, is now committed to a programme which will give access to many young people, at all levels of education, to a genuine understanding of Ireland, its history, literature, language and aspirations. It will encompass a broad range of disciplines from archaeology and literature to marine biology and politics. It will offer Irish Studies in an Honours BA combined course, as well as a part-time MA. There will be a regular programme of research seminars and facilities for visiting scholars. It is hoped also to provide scholarships. In all 23 academics will be involved.

16

Museums

The British Museum, London

Iron Age Collection

This consists of bone modelling tools, fired clay moulds, metal tools, fire-dogs, decorated bronze shields, bronze harness fittings, bronze sheath plate, iron scabbard, decorated bronze brooches, decorated bronze scabbards, gold torcs, bronze masks, piece of tattooed skin from a human arm, bronze pins, bronze and jet bracelets, bronze armlets, glass bead necklace, gold bracelet, pottery, bronze bucket, bronze mirror, iron spearhead, dagger sheaths, bronze scabbard plates, iron sword blade, bronze helmets, bronze shield bosses, model of a chariot, bronze and iron harness, bronze horse bits, bronze horse head piece, bronze figurines, and bronze spoons.

National Museum of Wales, Cardiff

Early Iron Age Collection

The following are in the collection:

Gold plated bowl, bronze cauldron, part iron sword, bronze hanging bowl, part bronze shield, embossed bronze sheeting, bronze terrets, several hoards, bronze harness fittings, bronze looped socketed axe, bronze sword, pottery, iron sword blades, iron fire-dog, part bronze bowl, silver, copper and gold coins, amber and glass beads, stone spindle whorls, stone mould, parts of crucibles for bronze smelting, bronze tweezers, bronze ring, silver wire bracelet, iron knife blade, bronze needle, harness ring, rampart vitrified material, spiral bronze finger ring, iron pen-annular brooch, sandstone cult pillar, carved pebble, bridal bits, gang chain, iron bars, bone and antler tools, stone querns and rubbers, tin plated bronze discs, zinc alloy plaque, bronze collars and coins.

Recent Important Discoveries

Hallstatt (Austria)

The name Hallstatt derives from the Celtic 'Hall' – salt, and *statt* – place. The picturesque village of Hallstatt lies on the lakeside of the Hallstätter See, surrounded by mountains and is one of the many lakes in the district of Salzkammergut.

Dr Joseph Ratzenböck, Governor of the province of Upper Austria, during one of his world tours, visited a museum in Beirut, and on a large wall map depicting the world in 1,000 BC found that in Central Europe it was blank except for a single dot marked 'Hallstatt'.

This small salt-mining centre was once the beginning of an epoch in the history of mankind. The early Iron Age (800–400 BC) is known as the Hallstatt Period, as in Hallstatt the richest prehistoric finds north of the Alps were made. What we know of this period is due to the archaeological finds there.

In 1846, Johann Georg Ramsauer (1797–1876), Director of the Hallstatt State Salt Mine, discovered on the hillside above the village, just above the tree line 300 mts above Hallstatt, in the lower end of the Salzberg high valley, a large area of grassy mounds, which in fact proved to be a huge prehistoric cemetery, containing about 2,500 graves. The graves were found one to one and a half metres below the surface on a stamped bottom, and some upon a trough of burned clay. Stones served as cover plates. 55% were inhumation and 45% cremation, with rich findings, 800–300 BC. The ashes were mixed with charcoal. Isidor Engl made many watercolour drawings of the open graves.

Being curious, the Director began to excavate them, and between 1846 and 1863 investigated nearly 1,000 of them. The cremation graves showed rich grave furnishings, indicating a ruling class, while the uncremated dead were poorly endowed. A certain system of burial customs can be derived from the arrangement of the warrior graves on the edge of the cemetery, and these had weapons. The graves without weapons lay in the middle section.

The last grave to be used (grave 994) contained a Celtic sword. It ceased to be used by 350 BC.

In 1876, hearing of the work of J. G. Ramsauer, on the cemetery, the Academy of Sciences in Vienna despatched a team to Hallstatt, and thoroughly investigated the workings in the salt mine. Here they found various remains of the Celtic miners, such as fragments of clothing, gloves, a leather hat, leather shoes, a salt carrying type of rucksack, bits of pottery, wooden spoons and plates, and remains of food and fruit.

It is thought this Celtic settlement dated back to 800 BC and became prosperous through the use and trading of salt, and salt

Hallstatt pottery

From Hallstatt

preserved meat and fish, which were despatched as far as Italy and Bohemia.

This chance discovery revealed a long lost culture, which for convenience sake was called the 'Hallstatt Culture'. For the first time it became known that besides other ancient cultures could now be added a further one – the Celts.

The investigation of the graves brought to light many iron made artefacts, such as magnificently ornamented weapons, brooches, belt clasps, horse trappings and domestic vessels, all made to a very high standard of workmanship, and many items beautifully decorated. This was the sign of a flourishing society with a high standard of living, due to just one commodity – salt.

This was mined in the Salzberg mountain, to which now access is given by cable car, as well as to the Celtic burial ground. Miners were extracting salt here over 2,500 years ago. The salt mines are still used, and they are also a tourist attraction.

The first settlers to arrive in this valley came 4,500 years ago and possibly discovered the salt. The Romans came too, and had a small settlement near the lakeside (50–390 AD), probably attracted

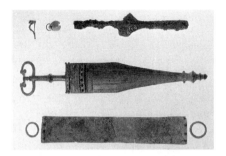
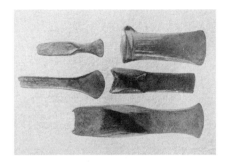

From Hallstatt

by the salt. It was partly destroyed in 171 AD by German raiders. Articles produced by the Romans, Greeks and Etruscans found their way to Hallstatt.

In the Prehistoric Museum at Hallstatt are housed many of the Celtic artefacts found in the graves and in the salt mine. The rest

Hallstatt miner

went to the *Naturhistorischen* Museum, Vienna. The following are in the Hallstatt Museum collection – iron weapons and tools, bronze ornaments, swords, pottery, grave furnishings, jewellery. From the salt mine there is a wooden bowl, wooden supports, fabric, pine torch, a salt-carrying rucksack and part of a log hut, found in 1877. Finds from the Dammwiese are pottery, jewellery and wooden parts. There is also a collection of coins, and water-colour drawings of the graves and their contents by Isador Engl.

The Museum was founded in 1884 and the first custodian was Isador Engl. Friedrich Morton was custodian from 1925 to 1967 and he excavated on the Salzberg and on the Roman site. Between 1937 and 1939 he found a further 60 rich graves apart from the cemetery. Due to the continued increase of the collection larger premises were found in 1969. The Museum has 30,000 visitors a year. Franz Zahler was custodian from 1967 to 1978 and he was responsible for the arrangement of the collection in the present premises. The finds from 1,300 graves are in museums. Karl H. Wirobal is the present custodian.

Rucksack

Leather cap

In 1734 the body of a prehistoric miner was discovered in the saltmine, evidently he had been trapped in a mining accident. The body had been preserved by the salt.

Mining activities in the last century BC were proved by excavations in 1887/89 and 1936/7 on the Dammwiese, situated in the upper end of the Salzberg high valley 1,400 metres high. A large Celtic manufactury, probably for salt making was excavated there. (Modern salt mining began in 1311 AD.)

The Celtic miners ate barley and beans, and apples and cherries, and they carried their food in wooden buckets. They used faggots made out of wood shavings for light, and ladders to climb up and down the galleries. In 1939 a salt-carrying rucksack was found in the saltmine, made out of leather and wood, and specially constructed so that it could be emptied without being removed.

With the salt the Celts of Hallstatt were able to trade for weapons from south Germany, bronze vessels from the Danube Valley, glass from north Adria and ivory from Africa, through traders in Italy. The mine workings went 300 mts deep and about 3,750 mts long and comprised three areas of workings. The miners

The Hallstatt Period in Chronology

Years BC				
2,000,000	Stone Age		Palaeolithic Age (Early Stone Age)	
12,000			Mesolithic Age (Middle Stone Age)	
6,000			Neolithic Age (Late Stone Age)	
1,800	Bronze Age	A	Early Bronze Age	
		B		
1,500			Middle Bronze Age	
		C		
		D	Urnfield Culture	
1,000	Early Iron Age (Hallstatt Period)	A		
		B	Hallstatt Culture	Holding time of the Hallstatt burial site
		C		
		D		
500	Late Iron Age (La Tène Period)	A	La Tène Culture	
		B		
		C		
		D		
0				

broke up the saltrock and, shovelling it with wooden shovels into their rucksacks, carried it up to the surface. Their rucksacks held about 45 kg. The miners clothes were made from leather and fur and their picks were made of wood or bronze.

About 400 BC the workings became flooded and unworkable.

On this account salt was extracted at Hallein, near Salzberg. Here in 1573 and 1616 ancient bodies were found. In the saltmine in Hallstatt there was a serious roof fall in 1734 and it was after this that the body of the Celtic miner was found.

In 1284 the Rudolfsturm was built above Hallstatt as a protection for the saltmine. It is now used as an hotel.

The rocksalt in the mountain was formed about 190 million years ago. At one time it used to be transported by women who carried it on their backs, also by horse drawn sledges, and until 1872 by boats.

La Tène (Switzerland)

Whilst J. G. Ramsauer was investigating the Celtic cemetery in Hallstatt, in Switzerland, another important discovery was made in 1858 at La Tène (the shallows), on a site on the River Thielle, near Lake Neuchâtel, which had sunk to an unusually low level and revealed ancient timbers.

When archaeologists from Zurich examined the site they found in the mud a large collection of beautifully made objects, as well as axes and axe heads, scissors, chains and knives etc., made by Celtic craftsmen who had occupied this area for many centuries, between 600 and 100 BC.

Their community was not as old as Hallstatt, but had improved on its culture, and had produced a much more finely decorated metalwork. This was the second great cultural period of the Celts, which spread right across Europe, and became known as the 'La Tène Culture'.

The La Tène Celts reached their greatest height in artistic expression, as well as their greatest wealth and power. It is not known whether this was the site of a votive offering or not.

In 1923, Paul Vouga wrote a *Monographie de la Station Publiée au Nom de la Commission des Fouilles de la Tène*, with over 50 illustrations.

Hochdorf

This site is near Eberdingen, Ludwigsburg, in Baden-Württemberg, West Germany.

In 1968 Dr Jörg Biel of the Archaeological Department, Stutt-

126

gart, received a telephone call from Renate Leibfried, a teacher and amateur archaeologist, of Hochdorf, reporting a tumulus in a field in that area. However, it was to be another ten years before it was investigated by the Ancient Monuments Department of Baden-Württemberg, Stuttgart, in 1978/9, led by Dr Jörg Biel.

It was found to be the grave of a Celtic Prince or Chieftain, which had never been disturbed previously. It proved to be a two-roomed wooden burial chamber, which had originally been walled and roofed by oak beams and covered by earth under which were about 50 tons of stones. In time the weight of the stones and deterioration of the wood, caused the roof to collapse, and the burial chamber was filled with the stones and earth, crushing the contents.

The excavation work took place from the 5th June to the 30th November 1978 and from the 7th June to the end of November 1979, and in 1982 it was further investigated and in July that year it was covered over again.

The tumulus had originally been about eight metres high, and the outer burial chamber 11 m × 11 m, and 2.4 m deep. The man had been laid on a bronze high backed couch, the back of which was embossed with six dancing warriors and two four-wheeled carts with a warrior in each and drawn by two horses. The eight cast bronze legs of the couch were fashioned as female figures with castor wheels between their legs. The four front ones are 35 cm high and the four back ones 32 cm high. The eyes were inset with coral. The ears are pierced to hold iron rings. The covering of the couch had been made of horsehair, wool and fur. The body had evidently been preserved before burial, probably in salt, as the hair was missing, until the burial chamber had been constructed. It was estimated that the man was about 40 years old. He was six feet tall, a very big man with broad shoulders, and had well-worn teeth. He had died about 550 BC in the late summer period. He had been dressed in embroidered silks and decked with flowers. A birch bark hat, shaped like a coolie hat, lay near his head. Around his neck was a wide gold band and an amber necklace. He wore a gold armlet, and gold brooches fastened his cloak. In a wide leather belt, decorated with gold, was a decorated gold covered dagger of bronze. On his feet were shoes decorated with gold, but put on the wrong feet.

The walls had been hung with textiles. In a corner was a big bronze cauldron, with a capacity of 500 litres, which was of Italian make and which had held about 400 litres of mead. From the sediment 58 plants have been identified. The cauldron was 104 cm wide and 80 cm high and inside lay a gold bowl. On a wall hung a row of nine drinking horns. Above the couch hung a holder, made of wood and covered with fur, containing 13 arrows with iron tips and one with a bronze tip.

In the outer chamber once stood an iron-bound four-wheeled wooden cart loaded high with bronze domestic items, three bowls, nine plates etc. and hunting knives. Also found were iron nail clippers, a wooden comb, fish hooks, an iron razor, an iron axe with wooden handle, a spearhead, harness with leather, bronze and iron fittings.

All the remains of the grave furnishings were taken to the Stuttgart Museum's workshop to be examined and restored. The restoration work was undertaken by Ute Wolf, Peter Eickhorn, Benno Urbon, Peter Heinrich and Martin Haussman and it was not completed until 1985. What they had achieved was astounding.

Due to the passage of time and the action of ploughing, the hill shape of the tumulus had been much flattened. At one period it had been tree-covered and there were remains of badger sets. It could only be identified by being a stony area in a stone free surrounding, many wagon loads of stones having been removed by the farmer. An aerial photograph of 1968 clearly shows the outline of the tumulus, with a smaller one nearby.

Three other graves, inhumation and cremation, with grave furnishings, were found in the tumulus outside of the burial chamber. Evidence of an early Stone Age settlement was found below the tumulus. The tumulus had been surrounded by a ring of oak posts.

The floor of the burial chamber had a slope of 26 cm, and had been covered with oak planks, and the chamber was positioned north/south. The wooden walled chamber was surrounded by another one 7.4 m × 7.5 m, and the space between filled with large stones. After the chamber was closed by a roof of oak beams it was covered by stones. These were covered by more wood, which in turn was covered by another layer of stones, then a layer of oak beams resting on the west and east walls of the outer chamber. Above this was piled the fifty tonnes of stones, or thereabouts, with wooden inserts, as well as around each side, and then covered with earth, leaving a mound of about 40 m in diameter. The burial chamber was situated in the south end, and in the north end an entrance of block stones, 6 m wide had been built. Before the chamber was covered in, it would have been left open for about four weeks, until arrangements for the burial could be completed.

In the tumulus were found ashes, burned stone, tools, drops of metal, partly worked pieces of bronze and gold and old pieces of metal, which would seem to indicate the sweepings of a metal workshop.

To prevent the soil covering the tumulus from being washed away, stones were laid around the circumference and oak posts sunk a metre deep and secured with stones. The entrance was then filled in. It is estimated to have taken five years to complete the tumulus. The soil for it was dug up around the mound, leaving an open ditch. The complicated construction of the tumulus and burial chamber was to foil grave robbers.

After the burial chamber had been opened up much use of plaster of Paris was made to lift up large sections of the debris of grave furnishings, for transport to Stuttgart Museum. It took about a year to investigate these debris. Before the plaster was used plans were drawn and photographs taken. About 2,000 bits and pieces were collected for investigation. The excavation attracted thousands of visitors.

The decorated gold neck ring (torc) is made from sheet gold, weighing 144 grammes, the outside diameter being 25.3 cm, and the inside 20.5 cm, so it was big enough to be put on over the head. A piece had been roughly cut out of it, 5 cm long and 1.3 cm wide, but this was not found in the burial chamber. The reason for this is not known.

The gold-covered bronze dagger is 42 cm long. The bronze sheath is partly decorated and inlaid with coral.

A little bag, made out of material, lay on the man's chest, and contained three large fishhooks and iron nail clippers.

The decorated gold armband on the right wrist is 10.2 cm wide and 24 cm long and 0.5 mm thick, and weighs 75 grammes. It had been made out of sheet gold. The two decorated gold clothing fasteners lay on the position of the man's right chest. The decorated gold sheet that was on the belt is 33 cm long and 8.5 cm wide, and weighs 130 grammes and had been sewn on to the leather belt, which had disappeared, using tiny holes that had been bored along the edges. For the shoes, which had disappeared, a wide decorated gold sheet was around the ankles and a hoof-shaped narrow one on top of the shoes. The former is 35 cm long and 6.5 cm wide, and weighs 21.5 grammes. They had been sewn on and had large holes for the laces. The narrow pieces are 2.8 cm wide.

The gold used was panned and not mined. It is thought the goldwork was made in a workshop nearby, especially for the occasion, with the exception of the torc. The total weight of gold is over 600 grammes.

The man's head lay on a cushion made out of woven grass stalks. The couch was covered by a material with a coloured pattern. Of the nine drinking horns, one was a very large iron one with gold bands, 123 cm long and holding 5.5 litres. The others had been made from real ox horns, all of which had disappeared, and only the gold bands remained. The decorated gold bowl found lying inside the cauldron, is 13.4 cm wide and 5.4 cm high and weighs 72 grammes.

The four-wheeled cart, which was largely made of iron and bronze, was found in thousands of little pieces and plaster of Paris was used to lift them. The cart body was lifted in a block 2.20 m long and 80 cm wide, weighing 750 kg. The examination of the cart and its contents took about a year. The wheels were 89 cm in diameter. The iron tyres were 3.5 cm wide and 0.5 cm thick. The wooden wheel under the tyres was made in one piece, having been shaped by the use of steam, and was 2.8 m long. Those on the front wheels were ash and those on the rear elm. The spokes were of maple and elm. The cart body was 1.71 m long, and 68 cm wide, and 8.5 cm high. The floor of the cart was made of thin round ash poles. The shaft was 2.38 m long and the width at the cart end was 15.8 cm reducing to 7.2 cm. It was partly covered with sheet iron. The double yoke was 1.20 m long, and decorated by two tiny cast bronze horses, 4 cm high, near the middle. There was a thin wooden stick, 1.66 m long, with a bronze grip and a pointed iron tip bound around with strips of sheet bronze and used to drive the horses.

The material on the wooden walls of the burial chamber was secured by hooked iron nails with bronze heads. The material was made of wool, badger fur and flax, and it was woven in several patterns and colours. Many different seeds were found in the remains of the badger fur. Under the bronze couch the space was filled with twigs and plants.

The cost of the excavation was 440,000 DM.

In 1961 it was estimated that there were alone in Württemberg about 6,700 similar tumuli.

17

The Celts of Today

Wales

The Society of the *Gwyneddigion* was founded in 1771 to foster interest in Welsh literature, and the Eisteddfod was revived in 1789.

In 1856 a weaver and his son, Evan and James James of Pontypridd, wrote the National Anthem of Wales, 'Land of my Fathers'. The University of Wales at Aberystwyth was founded in 1872, and the National Museum of Wales in 1907. A Society for the Utilisation of the Welsh Language was founded in 1885. In 1886 the Young Wales Movement (*Cymru Tydd*) was founded but later collapsed. *Urdd Gobaith Cymru Fach* was founded by O. M. Edward's son, Ifan ab Owen Edwards. In 1922 he invited readers of *Cymru'r Plant* to join together in this club to stem the tide of anglicisation. Camps were established to enable Welsh school children to enjoy a holiday in a completely Welsh environment. The unsuccessful campaign against the Tryweryn Reservoir was a blow, especially as the village of Capel Celyn which was flooded had a distinctive Welsh culture.

In 1935 BBC Wales began at Bangor. In 1936 Saunders Lewis and members of *Plaid Genedloethol Cymru* burned down an RAF building at Penrhos in Llyn. In 1951 a Ministry of Welsh Affairs was created, and in 1964 a Secretary of State for Wales was appointed, James Griffiths. In 1962 the Welsh Language Society, *Cymdeithas yr Iaith Gymraeg* was formed. The Welsh Nationalist Party, *Plaid Cymru*, seeks separation, but in 1979 a large majority voted against devolution. In 1967 *Plaid Cymru* gained seats in Westminster for the first time, and Gywnfor Evans became the first *Plaid Cymru* MP.

The number of Welsh speaking people continued to decline.

1921	1931	1951	1961	1971	1981
37.1%	36.8%	28.9%	26.0%	20.8%	18.9%

In 1962 a radio lecture by Saunders Lewis on *Tynged yr Laith*, The Fate of the Language, led to the formation of the Welsh Language Society in 1963.

Several campaigns for official status for the language were successful. In the 1970s the main target was a Welsh television channel, but there was no success until Gwynfor Evans, president of *Plaid Cymru*, threatened to fast to death, that they achieved their object, and *Sianel 4 Cymru* was established.

The Welsh Language Act 1967 (27 July 1967) was an 'Act to make further provision with respect to the Welsh language and references in Acts of Parliament to Wales.' Whereas it is proper that the Welsh language should be freely used by those who so desire in the hearing of legal proceedings in Wales and Monmouthshire; that further provision should be made for the use of that language, with the like effect as English, in the conduct of other official or public business there, and that Wales should be distinguishable from England in the interpretation of future Acts of Parliament.'

The first Welsh medium school, a private one, was opened in Aberystwyth in 1939, and the first local authority Welsh medium school was opened in Llanelli in 1947. By 1982 over 10,000 children were attending Welsh medium primary schools. The Welsh Nursery Schools Movement, *Mudiad Ysgolion Meithrm*, was established and expanded rapidly. By 1983 they had grown to 401, with 100 toddler groups in addition. A total of over 7,000 children now attend these.

Welsh medium secondary schools were also established, and the number of subjects taken in Welsh increased. Universities and colleges followed suit and Welsh students formed their own unions. Adult courses in Welsh can be taken throughout Wales. There are Welsh newspapers. The old deserted village of Nant Gwrtheyrn, Gwynedd, is being turned into a residential language centre. Both the Welsh Arts Council and the National Eisteddfod receive grant aid from the Welsh Office. Music, orchestral concerts, opera, choirs and records are also conducted in the Welsh language. There is also Welsh folk dancing, the National Museum of Wales and the Folk Museum at St Fagans. The Literature Department of the Welsh Arts Council, Welsh bookshops and publishers support and encourage Welsh literary talent. Over the last ten years local Welsh newspapers have become increasingly popular.

In 1971 *Y Bwrdd Ffilmian Cymraeg* was founded to produce Welsh language films. In 1983 the Celtic Film Festival was held in Cardiff.

Gerald of Wales, who journeyed through Wales in 1188 recording his impressions, described Manorbier Castle, overlooking the beach near Tenby, as 'the pleasantest spot in Wales'. To commemorate the 800th anniversary of his tour, Cadw Welsh Historic Monuments organised a series of exhibitions and events at Cardiff, St David's and other places in 1988.

Cornwall

Henry Jenner (1848–1934) the 'Father of the Cornish Revival', wrote in 1904 a *Handbook of the Cornish Language*, and was instrumental in that year in getting Cornwall included as a member of the Celtic Congress, and in getting Cornish included among the many translations of John V.1–14, on the walls of the Pool of Bethesda, Jerusalem.

R. Morton Nance (1873–1959) founded an 'Old Cornwall Society' in 1920, and became the editor of the magazine and did an immense amount of research, publishing in 1929 his *Cornish for All*, and in 1938 a Cornish–English Dictionary.

A bardic movement was founded in 1928 and since then it meets at least once a year.

The Celtic Congress first met in Cornwall in 1932. The first Cornish church service was held at Towednack in 1933. Services have been held in 20 Parishes and twice in Truro Cathedral. During the Summer School and at Christmas there are special services.

A. S. D. Smith (1883–1950) published *The Story of the Cornish Language*, *Lessons in Spoken Cornish*, and *Cornish Simplified*. E. Chirgwin published *Say it in Cornish*. In 1963 a collection of hymns was published by G. P. White.

Extracts from *A Few Words about Cornish* published by the Cornish Language Board.

> Cornish is historically related to Breton and to Welsh as common descendants from the Brythonic branch of the Celts. It began to diverge from Breton in the 6th century.

134

However, the two languages still resemble each other in grammar and in vocabulary. For example –

Cornish: *Yeyn yn an gewer yn mys Genver.*
Breton: *Yen eo an amyer e miz Genver.*
(Cold is the weather in January)

Cornish continued as a vernacular in Cornwall until the end of the 18th century when the last native speakers died. The language of the 15th century is known as Middle Cornish, and it is from this period that we have the Miracle Plays, religious works in verse. In spite of the efforts of a group of enthusiasts living around the Mount's Bay district in the last years of the 17th century and the first decade of the 18th century, a group whose members corresponded with each other and collected specimens of the spoken language of their day, wrote in Cornish and attempted translations of the earlier literature, by the end of the 18th century the decline of Cornish reached its definitive point in the death of the well known fisherwife of Mousehole, Dolly Pentreath, who died in 1778. Traditional fragments lingered on even into the 20th century.

Not until the third quarter of the 19th century was there any further interest in Cornish. Then the 'Celtic Revival' inspired the publication by scholars of most of the Middle Cornish literature.

The revival itself is reckoned to date from the publication in 1908 of Henry Jenner's *Handbook of the Cornish Language*. Jenner, a Cornishman, was on the staff of the British Museum, and he had studied the Cornish manuscripts. He proposed that the language might be revived 'carrying on where it had left off'. Later workers realised that the quantity and quality of the 'last remains' were not sufficient to make this practicable, and therefore used Middle Cornish as the basis for Revived Cornish as it was called by the two leading revivalists, Morton Nance and A. S. D. Smith. This basis provided adequate grammar and vocabulary. The phonology was derived from the description of Late Cornish available in various authors, from Welsh and Breton parallels, and from the spoken English of West Penwyth. It is this Revived Cornish which is in general use today. In 1951 'Mebyon Kernow', the Sons of Cornwall, was founded in Truro.

The Gorsedd of Cornwall and the Federation of Old Cornwall Societies, both bodies founded in the late 20s, were the organisations chiefly engaged in the promotion of the language, but in 1957 the growing volume of work, in publishing books, in organising classes etc. was handed over to 'Kesva an Tavas Kernewek', the Cornish Language Board, which is today the body which carries the chief responsibility for these aspects of the language revival. In recent years, and at the suggestion of P. A. S. Pool, associate membership of the Language Board was instituted, and associate members form *Cowethas an Yeth Kernewek*, the Cornish Language Fellowship. This is now an independent body with close constitutional links with the Language Board. It is the Language Fellowship which publishes 'An Gaunas', a monthly all-Cornish magazine.

Other bodies which are more or less concerned with the promotion of Cornish, or with its study, are, – Institute of Cornish Studies, Nebyon Kernov, Flamank, Yeth an Weryn, Royal Institution of Cornwall, Cornish National Party, Dalleth (to help parents teach their children), Agan Tavas, *Kernewek Dre Lyther* (Cornish correspondence course).

Various events are organised, for example, church services at certain festivals, a residential weekend, and other informal gatherings to bring Cornish speakers together. Banks accept cheques made out in Cornish. The support of TV and radio companies has been patchy, but the increasing production of video material by amateur and semi-professional groups is encouraging. At the time of writing there was a firm promise to bring the Inter-Celtic Festival of Film and Television to Cornwall in 1990. Some families are bringing up their children to speak Cornish as their native tongue, and the organisation '*Dalleth*' exists to support such families.

A number of primary schools introduce Cornish at some point in the curriculum, usually as an optional spare time activity. There has been a public examination at CSE level for several years, and in 1988 a full GCSE examination was available. The County Council gives limited support. A recent estimate puts the number of people who have had some formal instruction in Cornish at around two thousand, but the number of fluent speakers would be limited to a hundred or so. This number is increasing as the emphasis is more and more on the use of Cornish as an everyday language.

Dr Ken George has carried out research on the historical development of Cornish phonology, research which gained him a doctorate at the University of West Brittany at Brest. As a result we are now able to describe the sounds of Cornish at its various stages with as much accuracy as we are likely to be able to get. Dr George has proposed a revised system of pronunciation and spelling which would incorporate this knowledge. Adoption of change as proposed would require the publication of an entirely new dictionary, something which is desirable in any case, but would not require the replacement of existing texts immediately.

The aim of those in the Cornish language movement is to co-operate in the promotion of Cornish as a medium of everyday communication. Some link the revival of Cornish to administrative or political independence, others see it in purely cultural terms. However it is viewed, the future of Cornish depends on the active support of the Cornish people themselves.

Wella Brown

The Cornish Language Board publish about 55 items in Cornish. These range from dictionaries, grammars, pronunciation and spelling, language courses, poems, plays, stories, Bible stories, gospels, prayers and sermons and novels. Also an LP record of Bible readings.

A silver treasure was found in 1774 hidden in an old tin works at Trewhiddlo, St Austell, dating from 875 AD.

When the *Domesday Book* was written up Bodmin was the only town in Cornwall. It grew up round the old priory founded by St Petroc, a Cornish chief converted to Christianity in Ireland.

Eastwards from Bodmin is the great church of St Petroc, the largest parish church in Cornwall. South of Bodmin is Lanhydrock, said to derive from a Welsh saint, St Ydroc.

Launceston was for many centuries capital of Cornwall. Near Camelford is St Teath. The parish church has a Cornish motto, *Galas Ragi Wetlow*, a straw for a tale bearer. In the churchyard is a 13 ft cross.

Padstow was once called Petrockstow, after the Irish saint who founded the town about 550 AD.

Amongst the sand dunes near Perranporth is the site of the lost church of St Piran, marked by a cross. Founded in the 7th century it was the earliest place of Christian worship in Cornwall. With a shift of sand the walls were revealed in the 19th century.

Phoenicians came to Falmouth to trade for tin, and later the Romans, who knew it as *Valuba*.

Isle of Man

The Celtic period extended from 500 BC to 500 AD. Apart from the introduction of Christianity it would appear that Manx Society hardly changed until the Vikings arrived about 800 AD. (The Romans never landed on the Island.) The Island was well-populated during these periods, and there are many settlement and industrial sites. From the early Christian period at least 170 *keeill* (chapel) sites and burial grounds are known (some of the old burial grounds are still in use), and many water mills were also established during this time. Many wells on the Island, *chibbyrs*, were thought to have curative properties. The Manx language dates from the Celtic period and is derived from Irish and Scots Gaelic.

The first few centuries were unsettled and many settlements were established as defendable sites. Stock rearing became important on some farms, and new, hardier grain crops, more suited to the poorer climate and shorter growing season were introduced.

Metalworking and cloth-making were two regular activities. Locally made pottery went out of use by the 5th century BC. Some French pottery was used at a later period. There was little contact with Britain, but some jewellery made from jet, lignite, amber, bronze and glass were exchanged. The Roman occupation of Britain had little effect on the Island.

138

BAASE ILLIAM DHÔNE.

A MANX ballad on the death of Receiver-General Christian of
Ronaldsway, who was shot at Hango Hill near Castletown, 2d January
1662-3.

I.

QUOI yinnagh e hreisht ayns ooashley ny pooar
Ayns aegid ny aalid, ny ayns kynney vooar?
Son troo, farg, as eulys, ver mow dooinney erbee ;
As ta dty vaase, Illiam Dhône, brishey nyn gree !

II.

V'oo dty Resouyr Vannin, ard-ghooinney ny cheerey,
V'oo goit son dooinney-seyr as dooinney creeney,
As jeh dty ghellal vie cha row shin rieau skee,
Nish ta dty vaase, Illiam Dhône, brishey nyn gree.

III.

V'oo laue-yesh yn Earley, as sooill-yesh y Theay ;
Shen hug er dty noidyn gatt wheesh dy'oi ayns feoh :
She trooid farg as eulys ver mow dooinney erbee
As ta dty vaase, Illiam Dhône, brishey nyn gree.

139

It is thought that the first Christians came from south-west Wales. Consecrated burial grounds were established and later most of them had the addition of a *keeill*. There was probably a monastery at Maughold by the mid 7th century AD. It appears to have been a seat of scholastic learning, and may have had a library, scriptorium and mason's workshop. There is an inscription there to 'Branhui'. Part of the present wall at Maughold preserves the line of the original enclosure and the sites of at least four *keeills* are known. A fine collection of carvings have survived, but are mostly grave markers, but one dated about 800 AD was also used to record the water supply. At Maughold iron ore was exploited.

The administrative system was based on quarterlands, treens, parishes and sheadings, probably established in the mid-12th century. Modern farmsteads were probably built on the site of the original ones.

In 1977 Dr Gerhard Bersu excavated three Iron Age round houses in the farms of Ballacogen and Ballamorris, in the south of the Island. There is a small hillfort at South Barrule, a very bleak site. Originally it was a settlement of eighty huts surrounded by a rampart of turf with outer facings of slabs, with an outer defence of timber, like a *chevaux de frise*. Plain bucket or barrel-shaped pottery was abundant. Carbon dating suggests occupation to have been as early as the 6th century BC.

Dr Bersu also excavated three rath-like sites in a wet marshy area beside the Dumb River, about 1½ km west of Castletown. Two of the sites lie side by side, and are called Ballacogen A and B. The other is at Ballanorris 1 km away. There were three phases at A, two at B and four at Ballanorris. The outer walls of the houses were constructed of solid oak posts supported on the outside by a massive bank. Inside are sub-circular areas up to 27 m in diameter, and these were probably roofed over. Each house had a hearth, usually central, although one house had two hearths, around which was another ring of posts. One house had two squareish timber rooms inside. The occupiers of these houses were farmers, growing corn and breeding livestock. Radio carbon dates the sites to the 3rd century BC.

The only other similar timber house of that date is on Ballanicholas, where a ditch had been dug. The top of the mound was occupied by a circular timber building about 9 m in diameter. The house walls were constructed of upright timbers. The hearth was

Bronze axe heads – Manx Museum

to the right of the door inside. At a later date the house was reduced in size. A penannular brooch found suggests the late 1st or early 2nd century AD.

The sites of 22 promontory forts are known, and the majority are only large enough to take a single family. Only four have been excavated and these were re-occupied in medieval times. Close ny chollagh has a dump rampart on the landward side and a stone wall on the other three. It contained four huts. On a midden was a Celtic brooch. It would seem that the site was occupied about the middle of the 1st century AD.

1 km from Close ny chollagh is a fortified site on Chapel hill, defended by a rampart enclosing an area of about 4,500 sq.

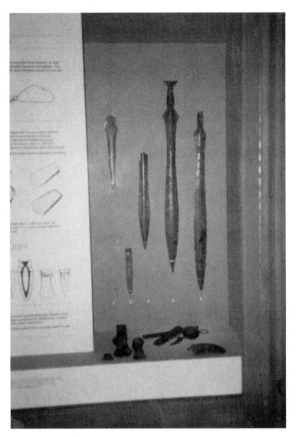

Bronze swords – Manx Museum

metres. Dr Bersu excavated here and found a Viking ship burial. The rampart consisted of a vertical stone face backed by a bank.

At Cronk ny merrice the defence seems to have been a stockade. At Cass ny hawin it was a rampart. At Cronk Sumark the inner of the two main ramparts is vitrified. The closest affinities of Manx Iron Age appear to be with south-west Scotland.

When the ruins of an early Christian chapel were being demolished in the 18th century on the Calf of Man, a portion of a decorated panel carved on a slab of Manx slate was found. It is thought to have been an altar front. The figure of Christ is flanked by the spear bearer, who would have been flanked by the sponge bearer on the opposite side. Above the outstretched arms would have been two angels.

The depiction of a still-living Christ, with eyes open and fully clothed in his robes, depict the link between the Celtic Church and the Eastern Mediterranean Christian Church. The panel would be a copy of a bronze prototype. This outstanding example of Celtic art dates from the late 8th century.

The 'Blakman' cross-slab of Maughold shows the arms of the Maltese cross decorated with lightly incised Celtic interlaced *triquetra* knots. The name 'Blakman' is in the top of the surrounding circle in Anglica runes. It is 8th or early 9th century. The concentration of early cross-slabs at Maughold shows the importance of this Celtic monastic centre.

The 'Branhui' cross-slab of Maughold is part of a plain cross-slab in low relief, late 8th or early 9th century. A square panel encloses an inscription in debased Roman minuscule lettering *Branhui, huc aqua, dirivavit*, Branhui led off water to this place, indicating the installation of a water supply. Traces of a stone conduit have been found. At Ballaqueeney there is a block of stone with Ogam script.

Manx was still spoken generally in the 17th century. In 1874 there were 12,000 Manx speakers. By 1901 it had dropped to 4,419. Ten years later that was halved and by 1961 only 160 were left. *The Book of Common Prayer* in Manx appeared in 1611, and a dictionary in the 19th century. Previously Bibles, hymn books and a Catechism had been published. A majority of Manx place names are in the Celtic Manx, a late evolution from Gaelic. The Islanders spoke a Brythonic Celtic in the pre-Christian period. Very little Celtic jewellery has been found on the Island.

Street names are now mainly bilingual and at the annual open-air *Tynwald* the law titles are read in Manx as well as in English.

It is thought that the three legs emblem could have come from Sicily, as its ancient name, *Trinacria*, means three legs, through the Crusaders, or through Edmund, who was offered the crown of Sicily by the Pope. Edmund was the brother-in-law of Alexander III of Scotland, who in 1266 became King of Man. The first known representations of the Three Legs on Man may be seen in an heraldic roll of 1275. It appears on the Maughold Cross which is 14th century. The Three Legs, or *triskele*, appear on the coins of a 10th century Norse king of Dublin. Ancient examples show the Legs running clockwise as the ancient pagan sun symbol. This symbol was also used from ancient times by the Celts. Man could be connected with Manannan, the Celtic sea-god, whose home the Island was supposed to be. The symbol also appears on the Manx Sword of State and the Seal of William de Scrope, Lord of Man in 1392.

The Vikings arrived about 800 AD and they ruled the kingdom of Mann and the Isles until 1266 and they founded the *Tynwald* Parliament. After a brief period of Scottish rule, the Kingdom of Mann passed to the English Crown. It was eventually given in 1405 to Sir John Stanley, whose descendants were Lords of Man for 360 years before it reverted in 1765 to the Crown by purchase. The Crown now appoints the Lieutenant Governor.

The *Tynwald* Parliament claims to be the oldest one in the world, with unbroken traditions and the Manx people have the power to legislate for themselves, with full control of their own financial affairs. It makes an annual contribution to Britain. The setting of the open-air *Tynwald* ceremony is the four-tiered Tynwald Hill at the ancient parliament field at St John's. On the 5th July Tynwald assembles for the promulgation of the new Acts of *Tynwald*, which have received the Royal Assent. The procedure described in 1405 to Sir John Stanley by the Deemsters (the Judges) as 'the Constitution of Old Tyme' is followed in almost exact detail today.

It is formed by the two branches of the Legislature in joint assembly with 24 members of the elected House of Keys, including the Speaker and eleven members of the Legislative Council, consisting of the President, the Lord Bishop of Sodor and Man, and the Attorney-General, and eight members appointed by the House of Keys. On the Hill, the Acts are proclaimed in Manx and English by the Deemsters. It is a recognised right of any Manx citizen to present a petition on this occasion.

About 1800 or 1700 BC Bronze Age people came to the Isle of Man. They had different burial customs and pottery, and could work in bronze. Individual burials under mounds were first used, the unburnt body laid within a stone lined grave in a crouching position on its side, together with a food vessel.

In the Middle Bronze Age cremation became general, the remains being interred in large cinerary urns.

Some burial mounds were placed on hilltops as at Greeba and Cronk ny Iree Laa. At the 'Giants Grave', Tynwald Hill, the large stone slabs have been exposed. It is thought that the Tynwald Hill may have been originally a burial mound. (When it was built up as a tiered mound some soil from every parish was used.)

Later Celtic people of the Iron Age arrived. Their greatest hillfort was on South Barrule (1,585 ft). Others were at Chapel Hill, Balladoole, Cronk Sumark, Lezayre, Castleward, Braddan, Close ny Chollagh, Scarlett, Cronk ny Merrin, Port Grenaugh, Cass ny Hawin, Malew, Burroo Ned, Rushen, and Langness, Malew. Cronk Sumark and Castleward had vitrified ramparts.

There are also more than a score of small promontory forts around the coasts of the Island. Some may date back to the 1st century BC. The sites chosen had cliffs on three sides and were protected by a defensive ditch and rampart on the landward side, as at Gob ny Garvin, Maughold, Cass ny Hawin and Close ny Chollagh, Malew, and Cronk ny Merrin, Santon and Burroo Ned, Rushen.

Celtic homestead sites were at Ballakeigan and Ballanorris, Arbory, Cashtal Lajer, Ballagh, Manannan's Chair, German, Ballanicholas and Braaid, Marown. An early Christian homestead site is at Port y Candas, Ballacraine.

The houses of chieftains were round, with a diameter of 90 ft, with concentric rings of wooden posts, which supported a low dome-shaped roof covered by sods. The hearth was central where the living quarters were. A wattle partition separated this area from the cattle and farm goods. Such sites have been found at Ballakeigan, Ballanorris, Cashtal Lajer, Braaid and Manannan's Chair. They were undefended and date from the 3rd century BC to the 1st century AD.

Christianity came to the Island in the 5th and 6th centuries and resulted in the construction of many *keeils* and crosses. The former were first cells for the monks, but developed into chapels. They were at first built of sods or wattle and daub. Those of the 8th to 12th centuries had stone-faced earth walls with a thatched roof and were about 15 ft × 10 ft and sometimes had an altar. They were usually surrounded by an enclosure, with a burial ground and the priest's cell.

Keeills can be found at Maughold, Chapel Hill, Eyreton, Balla-queeney, Lag ny Keeilly and Spooyt Vane.

Simple burial stones, with ogham markings, were raised in the 5th and 6th centuries and five have been found. Later simple crosses were erected from about 650 to 800 AD. In the 9th century

Celtic grave marker – Manx Museum

a more elaborate cross appeared carved on a tall slab, often richly ornamented with interlaced strapwork patterns.

These crosses are mainly preserved in the parish churches, but nearly one third of the pre-Norse crosses found on the Island are to be found in or near the churchyard at Maughold. Other important groups are housed at Lonan Old Church and at Onchan. Over 180 have been found. The early stones carried ogham inscriptions but later Latin was used.

Some of the finest cross-slabs are at Maughold, with one 7th century, one late 7th or 8th century, with an inscription to a bishop 'Irnett', one 8th or 9th century, with an inscription to 'Blakman', one late 8th or early 9th century, with an inscription to 'Branhui', one early 9th century with a Hiberno-British inscription

Celtic grave markers – Manx Museum

Crux Guriat, one 9th century with two seated monks, one 10th century at Onchan, with dog-headed figures, one 9th or 10th century wheel-headed at Braddon and one 9th or 10th century at Lonan, wheel-headed 5 ft high × 3 ft. wide.

St Patrick's Isle, Peel

The first missionaries landed here about 450 AD, sent by St Patrick of Ireland, and they founded the Manx Church. A century later St Columba of Iona sent further missionaries and the pagan Celts gradually became converted and gave up cremation for Christian burial.

In 798 AD the Viking raids began and St Patrick's Isle was also attacked. In the 10th century a round tower was built there. The ruins of St German's Cathedral are nearby, named after an early missionary. Work on it was begun in 1226 by Simon, Abbot of Iona, who became Bishop of Sodor. It took 200 years to complete.

In 1098 Magnus Barefoot, King of Norway, arrived at St Patrick's Isle with 160 ships and made it his base, building a wooden fort there, which was still standing in 1260. It was rebuilt and called 'The Peel'.

By the 14th century the Cathedral was in ruins and religious services had ceased.

In 1392 William le Scope, Earl of Wiltshire, King of Mann (beheaded by Henry IV), rebuilt the Cathedral, but it gradually fell into disrepair. In 1692/7 it was repaired, but by 1765 was already very much dilapidated again.

The crypt of the Cathedral was used for centuries as the Bishop's prison and many suffered confinement there. Conditions were so bad that usually seven days was sufficient a punishment. During 1656 to 1685 many Quakers suffered here. In 1780 the crypt ceased to be used as a prison.

Since 1982 archaeological excavations have taken place. Coin hoards, cemeteries and gold and silver ornaments have been found. This work has been undertaken by the Liverpool University Rescue Archaeological Unit. The St Patrick's Isle Archaeological Trust has been set up to help finance the work.

An early Christian cemetery, possibly of Celtic monks, and 8th century cross-slabs have been found, as well as the evidence of a village dating to over 2,000 years ago, with post-holes, hearths, loom weights, spindle whorls and whetstones. Over 300 graves have been excavated here. A circular Iron Age grain storehouse 9 m in diameter has also been found.

It has been suggested that Peel Castle is the castle of the Holy Grail of King Arthur, where he was crowned and where Queen Guinevere lies buried.

In the ancient Celtic folklore Manannan Mac Lir (Manannan Son of the Sea), ruled and protected the Island. He was said to be the great Sea God with magical powers and lived high up on South Barrule on the Island and gave protection to the Islanders in return for a tribute of rushes. At a sign of danger he would

The ruins of St. German's Cathedral, St Patrick's, Peel, I.O.M

enshroud the Island in mist and make it disappear. He also had the power to make one man appear as 100 men to deter the enemy. It is from him that the Island gets its name.

Even after Christianity had come to the Island, the Manx people retained their belief in the 'Little People' and food and milk and water would be left out for them. The Manx people believed that salt and iron had protective powers. Herbs, such as yarrow and vervain were also much used, for healing and protection.

In May sprigs of the eldertree (*tramman*) were used in the house, as well as twigs of the rowantree, which were tied in the form of a cross (*crosh cuirn*) and placed over doorways, and in cow's tails. The Manx proverb '*Mannagh vow claighty claighty nee claighty coe*', said 'If custom beget not custom then custom will weep'.

Celtic gaelic names which have survived are '*Balla*', a farm, '*Cronk*', a hill, '*Creg*', a rock, '*Keeill*' or '*Kil*', a church, '*Slieau*', a mountain, '*Kerroo*', quarterland, '*Claddagh*', a river shore, '*Carragh*', a marsh, and '*Niabyl*', a tail.

Many of the parishes are named after early saints. 'Bride' after St Bridget, Abbess of Kildare, 'Maughold' after Machald, 'Lonan' after St Lonan, 'Onchan' after St Conchen, 'German' after St

149

German (Karmane) the first bishop, 'Braddan' after St Brendan, 'Santon' after St Sancton, 'Marown' after St Ronan and 'Malaw' after St Maluoc.

Regular church services are held in the Manx language (*Gailck*). The earliest Celtic fiddle had a flat bridge and three strings, and it was in general use throughout the Island. Folk songs were also part of the life of the people. A festival of Manx Celtic literature, music, art, drama and dance, *Yn Chruinnaght*, has been revived and is held each July in Ramsey. In 1896 the Manx Music Festival was established to encourage Manx musicians. The highest award is the 'Cleveland Medal' (donated by the Manx Society of Cleveland, Ohio.) There is also a Youth Orchestra and a Youth Band.

Maughold Head (near Ramsey)

Legend has it that as a punishment for his evil doing St Patrick of Ireland cast Maughold adrift in a wicker coracle and that he landed safely below the headland, now known as Maughold Head. In gratitude for his delivery Maughold built a church near to the site of the present one, the latter being the oldest on the Island. Within its churchyard are the sites of four older churches (*keeills*), together with over 40 cross-slabs, Celtic and Norse, dating from the 7th to the 12th centuries. The Maughold Cross of red sandstone is elaborately carved, and dates from the 14th century, and was originally on the village green.

Sky Hill

The Manx Celts were defeated in 1079 by the Viking King Orry (Godred Grovan) at the Battle of Sky Hill, near Ramsey, and he ruled as King of Mann from 1079 to 1095.

In the Middle Ages the 'Three legs of Man' emblem received the addition of spurs and armour. Later the motto *Quocunque Jeceris Stabit* (Which ever way you throw me I stand) was added. The Manx Flag has the armoured legs in yellow on a red background.

On the Island can be found the native Manx Loghtan sheep derived from an ancient breed. Their fleece is brown in colour and they have four horns.

The Isle of Man is called *Ellan Vannin* in Manx. Caesar called it *Mona*, Pliny Monapia, Nennius Eubonia, the Irish Manann, the Welsh Manaw and the Icelanders Mön.

The Manx Gaelic Society, *Yn Cheshaght Ghailekagh*, was founded in 1899. Its motto is *Gyn chengey gyn cheer*, without a native tongue, without a nation.

There are about 60 fluent Manx speakers at present, all of whom have learned the language from English, as the last native Manx speaker died in 1974. He was Ned Maddrell of Cregneash.

The Society publishes a monthly bilingual Newsletter, and an all-Manx quarterly magazine called *Fritlag* is published privately. The Society also publishes about 29 items, which range from *The First Thousand Words in Manx*, a dictionary, place names, idioms and phrases, conversational Manx, a picture book, a language course, St John's Gospel, folk music and songs, hymn book, tales and stories, Old Testament stories, a sermon, Gaelic names of flora, children's books and colour books, also posters. Several are bilingual. There are also cassettes and records on conversational Manx, and old native Manx Gaelic speakers. A course of lessons in Manx, entitled *Abbyr Shen*, was broadcast on Manx Radio in 12 weekly lessons in 1987. A set of three cassettes and a book of these is available at £14.95. Evening classes are also arranged.

Mr Douglas Fargher and a little band of young men and women went about the Island searching for old folk who still spoke Manx and learning it from them. Eventually they were able to take tape recordings. He was the moving spirit in reviving *Yn Cheshaght Ghailckagh* and worked for 30 years compiling his English–Manx Dictionary, which was produced in 1979. He also arranged the Manx lessons for Manx Radio.

An annual public lecture is arranged, a stall is held at the *Tynwald* Fair and fund raising events are held.

The Orkney Islands

Early Celts settled on different islands in the Orkneys.

There is an Iron Age settlement and broch at Burran, North Ronaldsay, an Iron Age house is on the Calf of Eday, the main house being a large roundhouse with radial internal divisions, and dates from the last few centuries BC. A partly-excavated broch is on Lamb Ness, Stronsay. Three brochs are at Midhows, Ronsay. A first century BC settlement is at Brough of Gurness, Evis, Mainland. At Tankerness House Museum, Kirkwall, the complete Story of Orkney from pre-historic times to the present day can be seen. Old St Mary's Church, South Ronaldsay, is the site of a Celtic chapel.

In the summer of 1986 archaeologists from the University of Bradford excavated a site at Tofts Ness on Sanday, and discovered a late Bronze Age house, still standing to a height of over one metre, and still containing some of its original stone furniture.

The team spent eight weeks on the site and took several thousand items back to the University for analysis. It is estimated that the house dates from 700 to 1,000 BC. This find is regarded as of great significance, as the majority of Bronze Age finds have been of burial sites and very few have been of settlements. Due to its remarkable state of preservation much information has been gained about life in Bronze Age Orkney.

The circular house had been filled with wind-blown sand and it is thought that because of this the house had been abandoned. When the sand was cleared away it was found that there were five rectangular boxes about two metres long, which when filled with straw or other materials could be used as beds. In the centre of the house is a stone-flagged hearth. Peat deposits were found in the house.

Among the items being examined at Bradford University are pottery, flint, stone tools and axes, seeds and a plough. Plough marks were found. In the midden next to the house were found cattle bones with knife marks.

The work was carried out on behalf of the Historic Buildings and Monuments branch of the Scottish Development Department. It was a rescue operation on account of agricultural improvements and the damage caused by rabbits. Further work will be made.

The Shetland Islands

In 1958 a party of students from Aberdeen University, under A. C. O'Dell, Professor of Geography, were excavating on the site of a Celtic chapel and cemetery, dedicated to St Ninian, on St Ninian's Isle. The buildings were demolished after 1744. (In the graveyard in 1876 was found a stone 2 ft 6½ in. × 10½ in. inscribed in

152

Ogam script, and this is now in the National Museum, Edinburgh.) The churchyard had been used for burials up to the middle of the 19th century. The excavations were being made to locate the site of the church and in making them many medieval and post-medieval burials were encountered and removed. In July 1958 a Shetland schoolboy who had volunteered to help was directed to dig within the nave. On his first day he turned up a broken stone slab, with part of a cross incised on it. Underneath it he found a hoard of treasure packed in the remains of a larchwood box, probably placed for safety below the church floor as a protection against Norse raids, which began about 800 AD, and it was never possible to recover it.

The hoard consisted of 28 silver objects, eight were small silver bowls, one a hanging bowl, a silver spoon, three silver-gilt cone-shaped objects, a silver-gilt sword pommel, twelve brooches mainly silver-gilt, a silver implement and the jawbone of a porpoise. All the silverware was elaborately decorated.

The small bowls measured between 5.1 in. and 5.9 in. The hanging bowl had three rings held by the necks of three animals riveted to the bowl. The silver spoon has a tiny dog's head attached to the junction of the bowl, its eyes are blue glass and its tongue is out licking the bowl. There are three decorated cast silver-gilt thimble shaped objects, the largest of which is 1.75 in. high. Their use is unknown. The cast silver-gilt sword pommel is decorated with animals and its height is 2.15 in. The two cast silver chapes are highly decorated, one is 3.5 in. wide, the other 3.2 in. and they were made to fit on the end of sword scabbards. One bears Latin inscriptions, *Innomineds*, on one side and *Resadfiliscio* on the other. The 12 brooches are all penannular and are mostly cast silver-gilt. Each is decorated elaborately and differently. They were used to fasten clothing and cloaks. They have settings of coloured glass.

Two-piece clay moulds would be used. Such moulds, albeit in fragments, have been found on the Brough of Birsay, Orkney.

It is thought most of the articles in the hoard could be Pictish, and the hoard has been described as 'the most important single discovery in Scottish archaeology'.

The treasure was claimed by the Crown as Treasure Trove and deposited in the National Museum of Antiquities of Scotland, Edinburgh. Replicas were placed in the Shetland Museum,

153

Lerwick. The silver objects are made of very impure silver, some being over 60% copper.

Jarlshof

This is situated on the west shore of Sumburgh Head, which is the most southerly point of Shetland, 35 km south of Lerwick, and is one of the most remarkable archaeological sites in the British Isles. Here are the remains of several settlements, commencing with the Bronze Age, then Early Iron Age, Iron Age, Late Iron Age, Early Viking, Late Viking and Medieval and later.

During the Iron Age numerous stone-built brochs were built along the northern coasts and on the Scottish Islands. Other buildings were added until the Vikings came in the late 8th or early 9th century. They founded their settlement and expanded it until the 12th/13th century, when it declined. This was replaced by a medieval farmstead, which in turn was eventually abandoned. In the late 16th century 'de Laird's House', or 'Jarlshof', was built.

The southern half of the site became eroded by the sea. The site was first investigated between 1897 and 1905 by Mr Robert Bruce, after violent storms revealed massive walls, and part of the Iron Age settlement, a broch and wheelhouse dwellings were located. Further discoveries were made in 1925, when the site came under the Commissioners of HM Works. When it was explored by Dr A. O. Curle between 1931 and 1935, Late Bronze Age and Early Iron Age settlements were found. Between 1937 and 1939 Professor V. G. Childe and Miss B. Laidler made further investigations. Dr J. S. Richardson discovered the Viking settlements between 1936 and 1939. Finally the Ministry of Works completed the exploration between 1949 and 1952.

In the Late Bronze Age a hamlet of six houses, surrounded by a wall, was established. These people had sheep and cattle and grew the grain here, which they ground in trough querns. They also used fish, shellfish, seals and wildfowl. They made pottery, used stone implements and slate shovels. A bronzesmith from Ireland had set up a workshop and used clay moulds to make axes, swords and gouges, etc. Shortly afterwards new migrants built large circular stone huts divided into several compartments around a central hearth. Earth houses were attached and were probably used for storerooms. Iron slag was found on the hearths.

The houses became inundated with sand, more migrants arrived, and built forts, and the strong circular fort at Clickhimin. Later migrants erected a massive broch, 29 ft 6 in. in diameter, with walls at the base 17 ft thick, and it was probably 40 ft high, and a courtyard in the last century BC, or first century AD. (During this period hundreds of brochs were built in the Western Isles, the Orkneys and northern coasts of Scotland.) Large oval houses were erected in this courtyard.

These people had sheep, cattle, pigs and ponies. They too grew bere and ground it in saddle-shaped querns. They knew about iron but still used stone and bone implements. More migrants arrived in the 2nd and 3rd centuries AD and built wheel houses. They made a hard red pottery. They used the field system and had rotary querns, and saw-edged tools to detach the ears of the grain. New wheel houses were built until the courtyard was filled and areas outside it were built upon.

Christian missionaries established themselves on the islands during the 8th century. Viking settlers arrived in the early 9th century.

Iceland

The earliest archaeological finds indicate human habitation dates from about 300 AD, but some scholars maintain that the country had been known 600 years earlier.

Pytheas, the geographer, explored NW Europe in the 4th century BC. Parts of his works survived and are written about by later scholars, particularly by the geographer Strabo, who lived about the time of Christ's birth. Pytheas mentioned a country called Thule, six days sailing time north of Britain, and near the frozen sea, and that the sun stayed above the horizon all night in summer. This would appear to be Iceland, but it is thought it very unlikely that it could be inhabited so early in time. It has been suggested that it might be Norway, Shetland or Orkney, but the exact location must remain a mystery. Even so, the name Thule was used for Iceland even after it was occupied by the Norsemen.

In this century three Roman copper coins, antoniniani, dating from AD 270–305, were found in eastern Iceland, two in the ruins of a Norse farmhouse, near Bragdavellir, and the other on the shore near Hvalnes.

The Irish monks would have read about Thule and would want to look for it. The Irish monk Dicuil, a teacher in France, wrote a book, *De Mensura Orbis Terrae*, On Measuring the Earth, and mentions the Faroes, and says Irish hermits had inhabited them for about a century and that before the Irish came there they had never been inhabited, but because of Viking raids they had depopulated them. The Irish eventually found Iceland, soon after the Faroes. (The Venerable Bede (d. 735 AD) also writes of Thule.) Dicuil said he had been told, about 795, by priests who had been on Thule, from February to August, that sunset was only brief. They said that one days sailing to the north was the frozen sea. The early settlements of Irish hermits were probably intermittent and limited in size.

The most reliable source is Ari the Learned's *Islendingabók, Book of Icelanders*, dated about 1125 AD), in which he writes of the Irish priests settling in Iceland and that in the latter part of the 9th century, when the Norwegians began to settle there, that there were already some Christians there. The Norwegians called them *papar*, priests, from the Latin *papa*, father. As the Norwegians were heathens, the Irish left the Island, leaving behind Irish books, handbells and croziers. The handbells were used to summon the congregation and also to exorcise evil spirits. The croziers were carried by abbots and bishops. These were found in Papey and in Pappyli.

In the *Landnámabók* it states that *Papar* were living at Kirkju-baer (church farm) in the Sida district, SE Iceland. Other places are at Papey, a small island off the east coast, Papafjördur at Lón, Papafell (hill) in Strandasýsla, Papi, a deep pool in the river Laxá and Pappýli (Papar dwelling), as in the 'Hauksbók', being a district, in which there were two farms, probably in the Skaftafells-thing in SE Iceland. (The names Papey and Pappyli are also found in the Faroes, Shetland and Orkneys.)

The Irish hermits lived in small communities, each member having a drystone beehive-shaped hut. (In Iceland they had similar sheep shelters, called *fjarborgir*. Probably each settlement had a well, church and a garden. The *Papar* did not bring women with them, so settlements could die out unless new arrivals came. (They took sheep to the Faroes, for the wool for clothing.) The Norwegians reached the Faroes in the first quarter of the 9th century, and drove out the Irish monks there.

Iceland was fully settled by 930 by the Vikings 'in 60 years', both from Norway and Norwegian colonies in the British Isles, it is thought. Every man who left Norway to settle in Iceland had to pay the king five ounces of silver (land dues), *landaurar*. Many Celtic artefacts have been found in western and southern Norway, as a result of Viking raids. Many Norwegian settlers in Iceland brought Celtic slaves with them, and some of their wives were Celts, and historical sources relate of Celtic slaves rebelling against their owners.

Some Celtic personal names have survived, Avangr, Bekan, Bjollok, Dufthakr, Grélöd, Kadall, Kalman, Kjallakr, Kodrán, Kormákr, and Njáll. Celtic nicknames are *bjólan*, *feilan*, *hnokan*, *lunau* and *méldun*, which may have been baptismal names.

Irish Christianity in Iceland did not last. Cremation was unknown in Iceland. The sea going coracles (*curach*) used by the Irish monks were quite large, and had two or three layers of skin, and sails and oars were used.

The precious illuminated Saga manuscripts are housed in the Arnamafrean Institute, Reykjavik. The Sagas relate that it all began in 874, when the first settlers, Ingolfur Arnarson, found his seat pillars washed up on the southern shores of the Faxa Bay. He had them thrown overboard on sighting land to see where the Gods might choose a site for his settlement, and he called it 'Reykjavik', which means 'smokey bay', because of the steam rising. It became a village in 1750. Today's population is just over 91,000. Icelanders are a mixture of Celtic and Scandinavian origin.

When the first settlers arrived the only animal on the island was the arctic fox.

There are traces of Celtic influence in some of the Eddic poems, in personal names, and in the appearance of present day Icelanders, who have a higher percentage of the dark-haired type than any other Nordic nation.

The early blending of Nordic and Celtic blood may partly explain the fact that the Icelanders, alone of all the Nordic peoples, produced great literature in the Middle Ages. Recent blood group investigation suggest a closer affinity with the Celts in Ireland and Scotland than with the Scandinavians, Group O being predominant in Iceland and Ireland, whereas Group A prevails in Norway and Denmark.

The Saga Age was from 930 to 1030 AD. In 930 a General Assembly (*Althing*), was formed, and the Icelandic Commonwealth founded, comprising 39 independent Chieftains, and which lasted until 1262, when Iceland came under Norwegian rule. Christianity was adopted in 1000. The first Bishopric was established in 1056 at Skálholt, in the south, and a second at Hólar in the north in 1106.

In the late 10th century Greenland was discovered and colonised by the Icelanders, under Erik the Red, and about 1000 AD Icelanders led by Leif Eiriksson reached America from Greenland, but did not settle there.

In about 1100 the population of Iceland was between 70 and 80,000.

In 1380 Iceland and Norway came under the Danish king. In 1402 the Black Death reached Iceland and killed about two-thirds of the population.

When under the rule of the Danish king the last Catholic Bishop and two of his sons were beheaded, without trial, in 1550, and all church property was confiscated.

The population sank to about 35,000 in 1707/09 because of a smallpox epidemic, and again in the years 1752/7 and 1783/5, owing to famine, when it sank below 40,000.

At the end of the 1700s one Bishop was appointed, residing in Reykjavik. In 1880 there were only three towns. By 1977 there were 19 towns and 38 villages, where 86.9% of the population lived. Leprosy was at one time quite common.

Scotland

In about 1700 the Scots attempted to found a colony in Panama, but several thousand lost their lives there, due to the climate and disease, and the venture collapsed.

Scotland became part of England in 1707 when the Act of Union was passed. The clans were disarmed and stripped of their power, and the wearing of the kilt was forbidden. The SPCK set up schools in the Highlands using only the English language. The Hudson Bay Company enlisted many Orkney men to work in Canada, many of whom settled permanently there and migration continued until 1950.

The population of Scotland is 5.18 million. In 1971 there were 328 people who only spoke Gaelic. In 1981 there were 82,620

Gaelic speakers (bilingual).

Highland games, Scottish dances and bagpipes have close Celtic connections.

The Scottish National Party was created in 1934 and its aim is independence.

An Commun Gàidhealach (The Scottish Gaelic Society)

It is 700 years since Gaelic was spoken throughout the whole of Scotland, ranging from the crofter cottage to the Royal Court of the Kings of Scotland. Gradually the advance of the English into Scotland not only decimated the Scots, but led to the severe restriction of their language.

Although the language suffered, Gaelic culture remained intact, largely because much of the tradition, history and oral literature remained in the memory of the people.

After Culloden, the Gaels suffered ejection from their homes, together with clearance, famine, poverty and social and economic deprivation.

Over 100 years ago the Gaels began a political struggle in order to gain recognition through the statute books of the London Parliament. Although the first aim was to secure the rights to the land, it was John Murdock, editor of a Highland newspaper, who stressed it was just as important to strive on behalf of the Gaelic language and culture.

Although the Crofter's Act of 1886 gave a certain security to the Highlands and Islands, the struggle for the language continued. It was in this situation that *An Comunn Gàidhealach* was formed in 1891, so as to establish a general medium through which Gaels could come together in order to develop the Gaelic language and its culture. Other bodies had appeared and disappeared, but *An Comunn* has lasted, and has now passed its hundredth year of existence.

One of the first things *An Comunn* did was to establish the National Mod, and it was seen as an important avenue for Gaels who were searching for ways to keep the language and culture together. Today the Mod is seen as an annual competitive event. Its success bears witness to the vision of a revived culture and language, as seen and hoped for by those who established *An Comunn Gàidhealach*.

159

It attracted among its membership scholars who widened our knowledge of Highland history through long years of research. It preserved and extended, through the means of the Mod, things such as the writing of plays, the recording of old songs and oral tradition, encouraging the writing of literature, poetry and prose and it proved that the Mod itself is a continuing medium for those who are interested in the development of Gaelic. The Mod also offers an annual platform for new ideas and proposals.

In 1965 *An Comunn* took the first important step in engaging a full time salaried Director. Previously, although *An Comunn* employed full time staff, they were largely involved in general development work connected with Gaelic and in running the Mod. The new post was established through an awareness that it was by involving work on a professional basis with all that had to be done that notice would be taken of submission for financial support for Gaelic.

Since 1965 a tremendous amount of work has been done, which

has been the foundation for much which is now taken for granted. The following are only some of the developments in which *An Comunn* was involved, either directly or on the fringe:

Securing financial support from Local Authorities and from District Councils.

The first Gaelic Information Centre at Culloden.

Sruth, the first bilingual newspaper since 1908.

The re-establishing of Gaelic Summer Schools and Weekend Schools.

A White Paper on Gaelic based on the 1966 Census.

Establishing an office, and Director, in the Western Isles.

Establishing *Club Leabhar*, a bilingual book club.

Liaison with Members of Parliament on behalf of Gaelic.

Liaison with the 'minority languages' of Europe.

Reports to national and local bodies who could influence Gaelic development.

Writer's award at the National Mod.

Publication of books and pamphlets.

The establishing of 'Comunn na Drama Ghaidhlig', Gaelic Drama Association.

The establishing of CLI, *Comunn Luchd Iounsachaidh*, an Association for Learners.

The compilation of *Ghaidhlig BHEO*, a learners' course, in collaboration with the National Extension College, Cambridge.

Participation in the work of the European Bureau for Lesser Used Languages.

The staging of local community festivals.

Liaison with the BBC and IBA on behalf of Gaelic.

This list represents only a fraction of what has been happening. It merely illustrates that *An Comunn Gàidhealach* has been a means whereby much of what was for the benefit of the language was encouraged and established during this time.

Perhaps the prime achievement in general terms was that public awareness of Gaelic in Scotland increased. Particularly, many people concluded that Gaelic was part of their heritage as Scots and of their cultural identity. In order to move closer to their heritage, they began to learn the language, to the extent that it became possible to include them in the Census. This increase in the number of Gaelic speakers would have not taken place without the influence of *An Comunn*.

An Comunn has a structure which makes it the duty of Regional Councils to look after matters pertaining to the language in particular areas (Argyll, North Scotland, Southern Scotland and the Western Isles). Also, the Regions have been helping to unify matters. In the Western Isles, there is now a well-established Annual Festival in Lewis. Also in the four Regions, books, calendars, cards, cassettes etc., help to raise money and to awaken people's interest in Gaelic.

However, there is still much to be done. Since 1891 *An Comunn* has been in the forefront of the fight, working largely as a voluntary organisation, whose membership includes people who give selflessly of their time and energy for the good of the language. The National Mod could not be staged without the tireless work of volunteers at both local and national levels. The same is true of many of the Festivals and projects in which *An Comunn* is involved in the four Regions and in its many branches. It is hoped that many more people will decide to join and play their part.

Since culture is indeed the soul of a language, it befell *An Comunn* to work to extend the life of that soul in the years ahead. Although some may think that their grasp of Gaelic is weakening, it is true that they are Gaels in their hearts and minds. Therefore, the work of *An Comunn* is particularly important in the development of the language itself, establishing strong foundations on which can be built something that no attack can destroy. *An Comunn* will be working at parliamentary, national and community levels. We must not abandon our heritage nor abandon the efforts of previous generations to preserve it.

An Comunn's headquarters is at 109 Church Street, Inverness, where they also have a shop. They publish nearly 300 items ranging from dictionaries, vocabulary, language courses, correspondence courses, children's lessons, stories, tales, school books, novels, song books, posters, fiction, biography, essays, drama, Bibles, hymns, church history and bird books. They also publish prints, greeting cards, stationery, serviettes, badges, car stickers, tea towels, mugs, photographs, maps and a large variety of tapes.

Comhairle Nan Sgoiltean Araech (The Council of Nursery Schools)

This came into being in 1982 to provide Gaelic medium pre-schooling for children whose parents desired such provision, and without prejudice as to the linguistic or other background of the children. It caters not only for Gaelic speaking children but also for non-Gaelic speaking children. The majority of children entering CNSA Groups are non-Gaelic speaking, and in the majority of cases either both parents in a family are non-Gaelic speaking or only one parent speaks Gaelic.

In many ways *CNSA*'s nursery groups are similar to English medium groups. However, it has to ensure that its playleaders are not only conversant and can apply the general principles of good pre-schooling practice but that they are also trained in techniques of second language introduction. *CNSA* has to encourage its groups to meet as often as the local situation allows, with the ultimate aim of five sessions a week. Training is provided by *CNSA* and is conducted in Gaelic. Only Gaelic speaking personnel may take an active part within the Nursery Group. *CNSA* has the responsibility of ensuring a place for the non-Gaelic speaking parents in the overall organisation of the group, and to see that appropriate provision is made for parents wishing to learn Gaelic, ideally at the same time as the nursery group meets (but in a different room), and with the lessons relevant to what their children are learning.

Our Mother and Toddler groups present other challenges because they necessarily involve both the non-Gaelic speaking and the Gaelic speaking parents within the groups themselves. A whole new way of working for such groups had to be devised.

CNSA is also called upon to provide an information and advice service to parents on many aspects of bilingual family life, including the inevitable question from parents, 'Where will my child go after the playgroup?' Here *CNSA* liaises closely with *Comunn na Gaidhlig* who deal with the needs of the post playgroup children.

In addition to the nursery groups themselves, *CNSA* concerns itself with the availability of Gaelic-medium provision for pre-school children by other institutions, particularly in the field of broadcasting and the publishing of books and sound recordings.

CNSA is itself involved in publishing, having produced two cassettes and books of nursery rhymes and songs in Gaelic, a story book about the Gaelic playbus *Padraig am Bus Trang*, a set of ten wall posters, a cassette of words and phrases relevant to speaking with pre-school children for parents learning Gaelic, and a co-publication with Acair of a translation into Gaelic of the Usborne book, *First Thousand Words*. In broadcasting, *CNSA* is currently co-operating with STV to produce another series of programmes in Gaelic on playgroup activities, and co-operates with the BBC in informing parents of the transmission of Gaelic TV programmes for pre-school children.

Since the work *CNSA* is involved in had not, prior to the founding of the association, been attempted in Scotland before, except in individual groups working on their own, *CNSA* has had to seek advice and guidance from outside Scotland. The association has a good working relationship with *Mudiad Ysgolion Meithrin*, the Welsh medium playgroups association, and *An Comhchoiste Reamhscolaiochta*, the Irish medium playgroups movement, and consults them regularly.

In its first year, *CNSA* was run entirely by volunteers, with the only grant coming from the Highland Fund Foundation which paid some of the travelling expenses involved. The HIDE then provided a three year grant as the main patron of the association, and Highland Region's Gaelic Committee provided a grant through three years to employ a local field worker. *CNSA* began to receive grants from the Scottish Education Department in 1985/6, and this is now the main source of the association's funds.

Gaelic medium primary units have been set up in Glasgow, Inverness, Skye and Lewis. A Gaelic Pantomime is performed at Inverness. The Scottish Association of Gaelic Nursery Schools and Playgroups accept children of between 2½ and 5 years old.

The decorated playbus, a double decker, *Padraig*, was during the summer in Islay, Skye and Inverness, and in October in Stirling. During Skye Week several places on the Island were visited. In Stirling *Padraig* took part in the opening of the National Mod. At the Celtic Congress at Inverness, Padraig heard young children speaking not only Gaelic, but Irish, Welsh and Cornish.

Cor na Gaidhlig

Language, Community and development; the Gaelic situation. A report prepared for the Highlands and Islands Development Board, with recommendations for action. November 1982.

The Report Group has come to the conclusion that a new agency, of a radically different kind from those already in existence, is needed if realistic progress is to be made in further Gaelic developments. Such a conclusion has been prompted by several considerations which emerged during our study.

In particular, there is evidence of a great deal of fragmented and isolated effort in the Gaelic field, which, lacking co-ordination and frequently acting in ignorance of similar developments elsewhere, tends to peter out fruitlessly and waste resources.

We have also been aware of the fact that a number of bodies, particularly local government and statutory organisations, have a genuine desire to take positive action on the Gaelic issue, but do not have at their own hand the immediate guidance and expertise they need.

Accordingly we recommend the formation of a new agency, to be known as *Comhairle na Gaidhlig*, which would work at the interface between the linguistic and the social, cultural and economic aspects of development.

Our study has shown that an increasing number of authorities on tourism are of the opinion that a much higher Gaelic profile within the industry could prove a significant attraction to visitors. In fact, this is one area where Gaelic and its culture could be of definite commercial value if promoted properly.

We recommend a twin-pronged pilot project to explore two potential initiatives in youth activity – the one aimed at evolving group activities for youngsters in indigenous Gaelic areas, the other at bringing children from a non-Gaelic or fringe-Gaelic background into useful contact with the environment, with a possible spin off for the host community. We suggest that this initiative might be undertaken by a community co-operative, possibly by *Cochomunn Stafainn* in Skye.

We recommend that the Highlands and Islands Development Board, possibly in conjunction with another organisation or organisations, commission a study on Gaelic audiovisual provision.

There is room for a major annual Gaelic festival of a different kind from the long established National Mod, and Inverness would seem to offer the best venue.

The need for a popular Gaelic magazine or newspaper is seen as a long overdue development.

The Board of Gaelic Speakers should increase the appointment of Gaelic speakers to posts within the indigenous Gaelic-speaking areas and to obtain other posts which demand much contact with the Gaelic community.

The Board should advise the Secretary of State for Scotland of the need for a national policy toward the Gaelic language and culture.

A Conference 'Co-Labhairt 1985: Towards a National Policy for Gaelic' was held in Skye, when Mr George Younger, MP, Secretary of State for Scotland was present. The draft policy statement was submitted to, and accepted by, the Board of Directors of Comunn na Gaidhlig in November 1985.

The Conference recommended that education through the medium of Gaelic should be available at all levels everywhere in Scotland, and further important recommendations were made regarding Education, the Arts, the Media, Training, Government Services and Related Areas and the Law.

The 1981 Census

This census enumerated 79,307 Gaelic speakers, and in addition, a further 3,313 persons claiming to read or write Gaelic although unable to speak it. This represented 1.79% of the total Scottish population of 4,843,553 in the 3 plus age group.

In the Highlands and Islands Development Board area, less Shetland, Orkney, Caithness and Nairn, 20% of the population, amounting to 46,578 people were Gaelic speakers. Within the Highland Region 17,098 people, 9.5% of the population spoke Gaelic. In Skye and Lochalsh District 5,166 people, 54.2% of the local population spoke Gaelic. Strathclyde Region had 26,100

Gaelic speakers, 1.1% of the population, and in Argyll and Bute District, 6,408 people, 10.5% of the population spoke Gaelic. In 1891 the total was 254,415, 5.2% of the Scottish population. Since 1971 the rate of decline has slowed considerably.

Depopulation, and population movement, of Gaelic speakers into Anglicised areas, and non-Gaelic speakers into Gaelic areas, weakened the original Gaelic speaking areas.

Television in the Gaelic home is an erosive influence.

The refusal of the Scottish Education Department in 1981 to support the establishment of a bilingual project in Island secondary schools has caused some concern.

Cinema Sgire – a film festival has been established on an annual basis, moving among the Celtic countries. The parent organisation is called 'The Association for Film and Television in the Celtic Countries' and is based in Inverness.

An Comunn Gàidhealach has 56 branches, each of which must have a minimum of 12 members. The Western Isles Region has organised children's choirs, drama teams and helped in the publication of a periodical bilingual page in the *Oban Times*. Edinburgh is involved in a wide range of cultural and political activity, and publishes its own news sheet. Easter Ross mounted an extremely effective local campaign for Gaelic in the primary schools.

Stri (Strive) is a newish group with a small young membership active in lobbying particularly on broadcasting and education. Some members have refused to pay their TV licences as a protest about the lack of Gaelic programming, and they have been studying play groups.

COGA (The Association of Scottish Gaelic Students), began in the mid-seventies in the Scottish Universities and had demonstrations at the BBC in Glasgow. It has a membership of over 300 between Glasgow, Edinburgh and Aberdeen. There is a smaller activist organisation *Ceartas* (Justice), which has been involved in road sign daubing in the Highland Region and Strathclyde.

The Press

The West Highland Free Press and the *Stornoway Gazette* carry Gaelic columns and articles weekly and the *Oban Times* to a much lesser degree. *The Scotsman* carries a Gaelic article fortnightly. The bi-monthly *Today* in the Highlands and Islands normally carries two major Gaelic features. There are also student magazines and school magazines. Community newspapers carry small amounts of Gaelic material. All-Gaelic publications are *Gairm* and *Cruigean*. *Gairm* is quarterly, while *Cruigean* is a monthly supplement in the *West Highland Free Press*.

Amateur Drama

Increasing interest is being shown, especially in Glasgow, Lewis, Skye, Argyll and the Uists. A collection of about 250 plays are now at the Stornoway office.

There are three BBC Gaelic radio programmes which emanate from Stornoway, Inverness and Glasgow. There is also Radio Scotland VHF from Glasgow and Inverness and Radio Highland VHF from Inverness.

Television

BBC Scotland and Grampian TV give fortnightly programmes during the winter period.

The Church

In the Church of Scotland Gaelic services are dwindling, partly due to the difficulty in procuring Gaelic-speaking ministers. Only a few Gaelic students prepare for the ministry and a number of charges are vacant and Gaelic ministers sought. The 'Gaelic Essential' is changing to 'Gaelic Desirable', which usually leads to the appointment of non-Gaelic-speaking ministers. This church usually attracts non-Gaelic speaking incomers.

In the Free Church of Scotland more Gaels are members than any other church and it is not as susceptible to the anglicising influence of incomers. However, there is an increase in the use of English.

The Free Presbyterian Church of Scotland is the smallest of the three Presbyterian churches in the Highlands, but probably has the higher proportion of Gaelic speakers in its congregations than either of the other two, but is switching to English more rapidly than either of them. In Lewis there is the tendency to the morning service in Gaelic and the evening one in English.

The Roman Catholic Church

This uses Gaelic predominantly in the Western Isles with English only used occasionally. Due to the set order of service, incomers are more easily assimilated. They have no shortage of Gaelic-speaking clergy at present.

The overall situation is that old people in particular are being deprived of the language of their hearts, prayers and their religious fellowship.

Grant aid is received from the Scottish Office and the Scottish Arts Council.

The survival of the Gaelic language depends on the Gaelic-speaking community having a strong social and economic base.

Courses and Teaching Materials for Adult Learners

There are about a dozen course books and cassettes, also correspondence courses with cassettes, school courses and dictionaries, vocabulary and phrase books, grammars and computer software.

Courses or classes are held at Argyll and Bute, Ayr, Dumbarton, Glasgow (5 centres), Renfrew, Lothian, Kirkaldy, Dumfermline, Telford College, Aberdeen University, Dundee University, Glasgow University, Napier College, Edinburgh, West Lothian College, Bathgate, Crosswinds Community Centre, Tollcross, Edinburgh University, Lewis, Dunoon, Inverary, Furnace, Lochgilhead, Oban, Isle of North Uist, Aberdeen College of Commerce, St Andrews University, Airdrie, St Fillans, Crieff, Blairgowrie, Pitlochry, Stirling, Mull, Paisley, Cumbernauld, Helensburgh, Peterhead, North Berwick, Isle of Skye and Glenrothes. Classes are also held in London and Cheshire.

Weekend and Summer Schools are held at Skye, Edinburgh, Inverness and Wansfell Adult College, near Epping, Essex.

18

Brittany (Armorica)

Christianity was already there before the Breton invaders, who came principally from Wales and settled in northern and western parts of Armorica.

The pre-Breton populations (Merovingians), occupied the centre and eastern areas. Gallo-Frankish Armorica was made up of the territories of Vannes, Nantes and Rennes.

The Bretons were grouped in the federation of Domnonée, Poher, Cornouaille, Browaroch and Porhorët, which were broken down into parishes (*plous*), which became divided into *treves*. They introduces monasticism and their monasteries were mixed and women were allowed to give the sacraments. They were located in the Forest of Brecclien (Porhoët) and on islands (e.g. Ile Lavret and Ile Mondez) and at Dol, Quimper, and St Pol.

The Bretons advanced eastwards and took Vannes and pillaged Nantes. The Franks reversed this advance in 590.

Gradually the Bretons took on Frankish names and traditions, but they were considered rebellious and untrustworthy by the Franks. On account of their raiding practices, Charlemagne sent in troops in 799 and 811, as did Louis in 818 and 824.

The Bretons came under the influence of the Carolingians and the Benedictine Order came to Brittany by the founding of Redon Abbey in 832.

Norman invasions began to take place. In 819 they attacked the island of Noirmontier and the monks had to flee to the mainland. Finally the Normans were defeated at Questembert in 888 and Brittany enjoyed a period of peace until 907, when Norman raids began again, and in 921 the county of Nantes was ceded to them. This led to many Bretons fleeing to France and England, and for several years afterwards many monks left the area, but took their Breton culture with them.

In 936 an English fleet brought Bretons to Brittany, and they defeated the Normans at Dol and also at Nantes in 937 and Trans

170

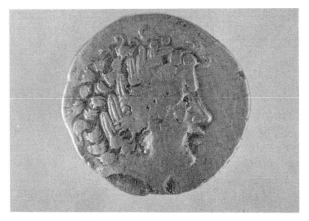

Gold coins of the Redones (120–110 BC) (Rennes Museum)

in 939. Thereafter reconstruction began but it took many years to restore the monasteries. Meanwhile the Breton language had retreated westwards. After 958 Brittany passed from the House of Nantes to that of Cornouaille.

Henry II, king of England, and Count of Anjou, became Duke of Normandy and took over the duchy of Brittany. The Celtic Church suffered during this period and eventually their monasteries came to accept the Benedictine Order and came under Rome and the Latin tradition. The Breton Church finally lost its independence in 1199 by the ruling of Pope Innocent III. The marriage of priests in the Breton Church had been common.

Gradually Brittany came under the influence of the new religious orders of the Augustinians and Cistercians.

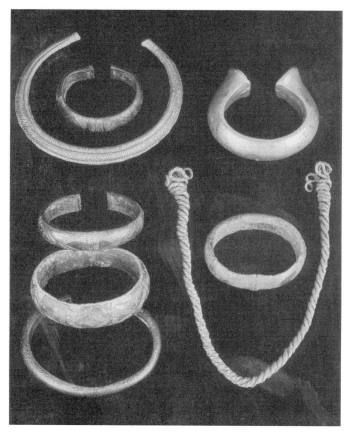

Gold torcs and bronze bracelets (Rennes Museum)

In the 13th century Brittany became closely connected to France and the bishops were mainly French. In Paris there was a *Collège de Cornouaille*.

In agriculture, whilst wheat was grown in the interior, oats and rye were grown in the coastal regions. Wines were exported to England. Herring fishing developed and salt and cloth were exported.

Following the Breton War of Succession, 1341 to 1381, and the Treaty of Guerande, the union with France was inevitable. The support of Edward III of England was sought and the Anglo-French struggle began. In 1372 English troops landed in Brittany. In 1378 Charles V confiscated the Duchy of Brittany and attached it to the Crown, in spite of violent protests. Revolts and pillaging

Bronze (Rennes Museum)

took place throughout the 15th century and by the end of that century the Bretons sided with the French against the English, although they still traded with them.

At this period the population of Brittany was between one and one-and-a-quarter million.

In 1453 Pope Nicholas V forbade the giving of a living in Brittany to a non-Breton. In 1460 a University was opened in Nantes. In 1485 a sovereign Breton Parliament was formed.

The struggle against the French Crown began in 1480 and in 1481 Brittany formed an alliance with England and Austria. However, in 1488 the Bretons were defeated at the battle of St Aubin du Cormier, but no help was given by England or Austria.

173

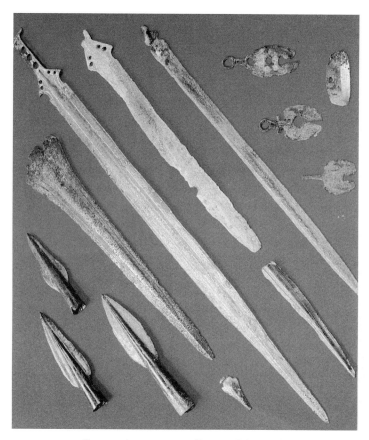

Bronze Age weapons (Rennes Museum)

The Treaty du Verger in August 1488 made the Duke of Brittany subject to the French Crown.

During the 15th century the textile industry grew and the maritime prosperity increased, and Nantes and Rennes grew, but the economy was still mainly agriculture.

In 1489/90 German, Spanish and English mercenaries landed to support Brittany, and a truce came in 1489 at the Treaty of Frankfurt. However, in 1491, there was a French offensive and the Duchy was occupied.

In 1532 the Edict of Union (with France) was published at Nantes. On the 15th August 1532 the dauphin François was crowned Duke of Brittany at Rennes and was the last to bear that

174

Breton jacket, Elliant, Finistère, 1910. (Rennes Museum)

title, as he died in 1536 and his successor, Henry II, regarded Brittany as just a province of France.

In 1554 a Breton Parliament was formed with 16 Bretons and 16 non-Bretons and after 1532 Breton bishops were replaced by French ones.

In 1582 the Governor of Brittany tried to lead a revolt against the French and did not submit until 1598.

Richelieu, when Governor of Brittany, tried to bring the Breton navy under French control.

In 1675 there was a rebellion in Rennes, Dinan and Vannes 'against the imposition of taxes by the French, as well as a peasant revolt, which ended in September 1675 on the death of its leader,

Part of Breton jacket, Pont L'abbé, Finistère, 1880 (Rennes Museum)

Le Balp. Rennes was occupied by 6,000 troops and some prisoners were hanged, broken on the wheel or sent to the galleys. 10,000 troops spent the winter in Brittany, but were withdrawn in March 1676. French demands brought financial hardship on Brittany. Some Breton Saints were replaced by French ones by some priests. In 1717 the French Commander-in-Chief of Brittany dissolved the Parliament and brought in troops. In 1720 four Breton nobles were executed for treason. In 1765 the whole Breton Parliament was summoned to Paris to be reprimanded, which resulted in 85 of the 97 magistrates resigning. In 1788 troops occupied Rennes and 19 Breton nobles were imprisoned in the Bastille. In 1790 the parliament was suppressed. In 1791 the *Association Bretonne* was founded, but was banned in 1858. In March 1792 it was ordered

176

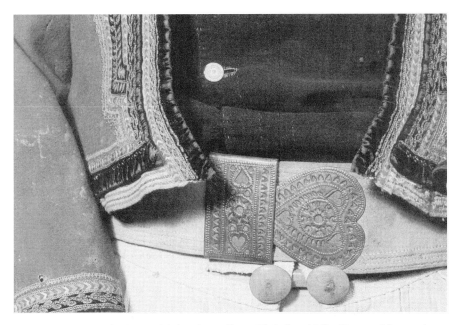

Part of Breton jacket and belt, Plomodiern, Finistère, 1850. (Rennes Museum)

that all objects of value should be removed from the churches, also that farmers' assets should be investigated and grain removed to depots. This caused unrest amongst the peasants, who also did not like the compulsory military service and were against the execution of the king. In 1793 there was insurrection in Vendée and guerrilla warfare took place. Revolt broke out in the Fourgeres, Vitré, Rennes and Redon, and the town of La Roche-Bernard was occupied. The French Government defeated the insurgents in December 1793 and brought in the Terror. A treaty was signed in April 1795, but fighting soon broke out again. 5,500 men were raised in England, including 1,500 French prisoners of war, and they landed in Brittany at Carnac in June 1795, where they were joined by thousands of Bretons. The French army drove them back, and the Bretons surrendered. There was further fighting in 1797, and religious persecution, and again in 1799. A truce was made in 1800 with Bonaparte but he broke it and sent in 60,000 troops. In 1801 there were further uprisings and Brittany was occupied. In 1830 an insurrection was attempted. Bretons took an active part in the 1870 revolution and raised an army of 60,000 men.

177

After 1870 the institution of compulsory primary education allowed the French to begin an attack on the Breton language. In 1898 the *Union Regionaliste Bretonne* was founded, but in 1911 there came a split, and the FRB was formed, but this proved to be just as timid as the URB. Other organisations were formed but made little impact. However, up to 1914 there were almost 150 Breton periodicals. Many militants lost their lives in the Great War. *Breiz Atas*, founded in 1918, was concerned with the preservation of the Breton language, traditions and costume but had little support. After 1918 there were many new organisations, and up to 1931 there were major changes within the Breton movement, and the question of autonomy was put forward, and persisted to 1939, together with the case of teaching Breton in schools. In October 1939 the PNB was dissolved and its archives burned.

The Vichy Government looked favourably on regionalism, but Allied landings in North Africa was the beginning of the end for Breton recognition. In the latter part of the war about 70 extremist nationalists formed a Breton Unit under the German Command. This led to severe repression on the whole of the Breton movement and, in 1944, to killings.

In trials which took place between 1944 and 1947 dozens of Bretons were sentenced to terms of imprisonment, from five years to life, and hundreds were sentenced to loss of rights. A delegation of Welsh people went to Brittany in 1947 to investigate the matter. Their conclusions were that, 'Consequently it is difficult not to conclude that the mere fact of having taken part in any kind of Breton activity was a sufficient motive for the French Government to indulge in persecution.'

Between 1954 and 1962 Brittany lost 100,000 people under 35 years through emigrations. In 1969 the average income in Brittany was equivalent to 80% of the average French income. Breton periodicals fell to 36 in 1950. However, there was a slow recovery of the Breton movement, and Celtic activities. Wrestling and fetes with the playing of the 'binion', bagpipes, and the 'bombarde', a woodwind instrument, grew in popularity. Breton scouts were formed.

In 1951 CELIB was set up to publicise Brittany, and published a monthly paper *La Vie Bretonne*. In 1962 railway lines were barricaded against new tariffs, and it campaigned against the closure of the last major sector of the steel industry in Brittany, but this was

178

closed down in 1966. However, the inability to bring about its programme caused a split in its ranks and it lost its vitality.

In 1956 POB was formed. In 1964 UDB sought to popularise the Breton language and published a monthly paper in Breton. It is a left-wing political party. SAV, another political party was founded in 1972. The establishment of youth hostels for Breton speakers was resumed. Breton Summer Schools were also established. SADED is an institute concerned with teaching Breton by correspondence. Attempts have been made to reconstitute the Celtic Church and Celtic monks are trained. There was worker and peasant unrest in the 1960s and 70s, when explosives were used. In 1972 there were riots. In 1974 the FLB/ARB attacked the TV transmitter at Roc Tredudon and it was destroyed by explosives. In 1975 there were further explosions. In 1977 the electricity board HQ in Rennes was seriously damaged and a further 33 bomb attacks took place. In 1978 the broadcasting studios in Rennes were wrecked and there were many other attacks.

In 1976 in primary education it was permitted to teach Breton for one hour a week if there was a demand for it. In secondary education it was permitted to teach Breton three hours per week if there was a group of at least ten pupils. Institutes and Chairs have been established in the universities of Brest and Rennes.

The French Government had tried in many ways to suppress the Bretons, e.g. by trying to prevent a pilgrimage, trying to prevent the addressing of letters in Breton, trying to replace *Radio Bretagne*, trying to dissolve the Navy's Breton pipe band, trying to prevent parents giving their children Breton Christian names, trying to ban the use of car stickers.

The cultural movement *Kendalc'h*, is concerned with music and dancing for young people. A traditional gathering *Fest-noy*, with music and cakes and cider, is increasing in popularity.

In a 1975 opinion poll 15% were in favour of independence for Brittany. *Skourr Breizh ar c'hendalc'h Ketiek* is the Breton section of the Interceltic Congress.

The separatist movement FLB (*Front pour le Liberation*) seeks self-government. Their motto is – *Hep Brezhoney Breizh ebet*, Without Breton, no Brittany. The PDG (*Le Poing dans la Gueule*) however is an extremist group.

The Bretons have their own national costume. In earlier times if children spoke Breton in school they were punished by having clogs hung around their necks.

Small local radio stations broadcast in Breton, whilst clubs, societies, theatres and publishers endeavour to keep Breton alive. Brittany has a population of about 2½ millions and probably about a third have some knowledge of Breton. The population of Basse-Bretagne is 1½ million of which less than half can speak Breton.

Brittany became part of France in 1532.

In Lorraine every August is a Bagpipe Festival.

Germany

There is at Bonn University, West Germany, a *Sprachwissenschaftliches Institut* which has published several books about the Celts, the titles of which are *Die Festlandkeltischen Sprachen*, by K. H. Schmidt, 1977, *Indogermanisch und Keltisch* by K. H. Schmidt, 1977, *History and Culture of the Celts* by K. H. Schmidt, 1986 and Prof. Dr J. K. Zeuss, *Begründer der Keltologie und Historica (1806–1856)*, by H. Hablitzel, 1987.

BIBLIOGRAPHY

A History of the Welsh (HTV4, 1987)

Altamira, R. *A History of Spanish Civilization* (Constable, 1930)

Bender, B. *Archaeology of Brittany, Normandy and the Channel Islands* (Faber & Faber, 1986)

Biel, J. *Der Keltenfurst von Hochdorf* (Theiss, 1985)

Clare, T. *Archaeological Sites of the Lake District* (1981)

Close-Brooks, J. *St Ninian's Isle Treasure* (HMSO Edinburgh, 1981)

Collis, J. *The European Iron Age* (Routledge, 1984)

Cuevillas, F. *La Civilizacion Celtica en Galicia*

Cunliffe, B. *The Celtic World* (Bodley Head, 1979)

Fox, A. *South-West England, 3500 BC–600 AD*

Hamilton, J. R. C. *Jarlshof Official Guide* (HMSO Edinburgh, 1953)

Hubber, E. J. *Cornwall Blue Book Guide* (1988)

Johannesson, J. *A History of the Old Icelandic Commonwealth* (University of Manitoba Press, 1974)

Kniveton, G. N. *The Manx Experience* (1988)

O'Callaghan, M. J. C. *Separatism in Brittany* (Dyllansow Truran, 1983)

Pearsall, W. & Pennington, W. *The Lake District* (Collins, 1973)

Ross, Anne. *Celtic Britain* (Routledge, Kegan & Paul, 1985)

Ryan, M. *Treasures of Ireland* (1983)

Stead, J. M. *Celtic Art* (British Museum Publications)

Stranks, C. J. *The Life and Death of St Cuthbert* (SPCK, 1987)

The Galway Guide (Irish Tourist Board)

Verdejo, X. L. L. *Galicia* (Conselleria de Turismo)

Wightman, E. M. *Gallia Belgica* (Batsford, 1985)

Any information obtained from the above is hereby acknowledged with thanks by the author.